AIR RAID—PEARL HARBOR!

AIR RAID— PEARL HARBOR!

The Story of December 7, 1941

By Theodore Taylor
Illustrated by W. T. Mars

Thomas Y. Crowell Company
New York

CONTENTS

To Christopher Robin
With a hope for peace during his lifetime

THE SPY SHIP

There they are, spread out in the middle of the blue-green Pacific Ocean, eight lovely, lazy, windswept islands called The Hawaiians. From little, lonely Niihau, the westernmost, to the big island of Hawaii, nearest the United States mainland, quiet peace and deep contentment reign in these gentle fall months of the year 1941.

True, wars are raging far away, in Europe and China, and one hears occasional echoes of these wars, but in The Hawaiians one listens more to the wind songs in the palm and flame trees. There is a South Seas magic in the air. By warm day and velvet night, the distant sounds and threats of war are lost to the laughter of the people and the soft strains of guitars, the moonlight and the tumbling clouds.

Of course the people of Oahu, the most heavily populated island, with Honolulu as its only city, do have daily reminders of a troubled world. They can see the great naval base at Pearl Harbor, and the grim warships that are constantly clustered there. They can hear the buzzing planes from the Army Air Corps base at Hickam Field.

The people also know that, of late, gun emplacements have been spotted around the island, and there is whispered talk of some type of secret electronic device up in the hills. It is on wheels and has a big antenna that turns.

But the ships, the planes, the guns, and that mysterious electronic "thing" on wheels, they agree, are simply to preserve the peace. What's more, no one would dare to attack the enchanted isles when all this equipment stands ready on Oahu—when the battleships, aircraft carriers, cruisers, destroyers, and submarines can sail out to defeat an enemy.

The people know, also, that there is an even

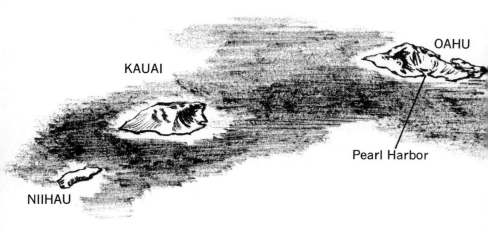

KAUAI

OAHU

Pearl Harbor

NIIHAU

greater weapon, not secret at all. It is as old as the islands themselves, as old as the Polynesian warriors with their canoes and their knowledge of the seas and winds. It is *distance.*

Hawaii is thousands of miles from the German leader, Adolf Hitler, and his soldiers, tanks, and aircraft. The dictator Hitler has dreams of German domination of Europe, if not the world. On September 1, 1939, his armies moved against neighboring Poland, causing England and France to declare war against Germany three days later. England and France oppose Hitler's plans, as well as those of his partner in war, the Italian dictator Benito Mussolini.

Already, though, France has been defeated by Germany, as have Belgium, The Netherlands, Norway, Denmark, and tiny Luxemburg. England is

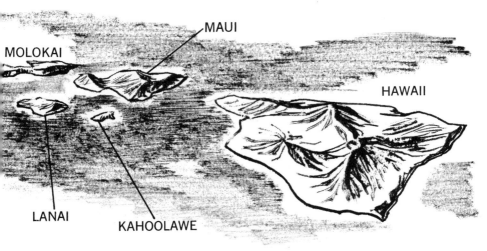

fighting on desperately, supported by her allies—
Canada, Australia, New Zealand, and South Africa.
Lately, the giant Russia has joined in the fight
against Germany. Hitler, now believed to be a mad-
man, attacked Russia in June 1941.

Yet these bitter battles being fought all over Europe, and even on the desert sands of North Africa,
seem far away from Hawaii. Closer is Japan, with
her strong, new Navy. Even so, almost four thousand miles separates Tokyo from Honolulu.

Besides, Japan is busy fighting China. Since 1931
Japan, off and on, has been sending troops against
the Chinese, determined to expand her empire in
Asia. Now Japan has established bases in Vichy
French possessions in Indochina, an area rich in the
raw materials she needs to feed her war machine.

Distance, however, makes the people of The
Hawaiian Islands feel safe from death and destruc-
tion, no matter what is taking place in Europe or
Asia.

But wait, isn't that a Japanese ship standing into
Honolulu harbor at this very moment—at 8:30 A.M.
on this first day of November 1941?

According to a story in the *Honolulu Advertiser,*
the ship may be the last Japanese vessel to visit for
a very long time. The name on her stern is *Taiyo
Maru,* and she looks a little weatherbeaten, as if she
has sailed rough waters. Rust streaks make ugly

blotches on her hull. Now she moves slowly toward Pier 8, near the famed Aloha Tower, landmark of the Honolulu waterfront.

Usually there is great celebration when a passenger ship is warped to the docks. It's the traditional way of saying *aloha,* which means, in Hawaiian, either "hello" or "good-bye." Hula girls in grass skirts dance amid a throng of happy greeters. The Royal Hawaiian Band fills the warm, moist air with music. Flower leis of carnations or pikake are draped over almost every arm.

But this day is solemn; and almost ominously quiet: no pretty hula girls with swaying hips, no booming band in splendid uniforms. The people on the dock simply stare out at the ship. In fact, the atmosphere is strange and somber, even though anxious passengers crowd the *Taiyo Maru*'s decks to watch the arrival, waving to friends and relatives.

Until recently, Japanese ships often called at the port, discharging passengers and cargo, sometimes taking on the island's sugarcane products or juicy pineapples. For years, the white flag with the red ball in the center, signifying vessels from the quaint Land of the Rising Sun, has always been welcome. Also, many Japanese have migrated to these islands, and now think of themselves as true and loyal Americans.

Once ruled by kings and queens, the Hawaiian

islands were annexed by the United States in 1898 and formally became an American territory in 1900. The first Japanese migrated to Hawaii fifteen years before that date. Most of them now living here have known no other home. However, many disturbing things have happened in the past eight months.

Serious political trouble exists now between the United States and Japan. No longer will Japanese ships be permitted to visit United States ports, and naturally, Japan will not permit United States flag vessels to call at her ports. The two nations, because of their political differences, have broken off trade relations.

Therefore, the story in the *Honolulu Advertiser* is quite correct. The *Taiyo Maru* will be the last ship from Nippon for a long time. Chartered to bring stranded passengers home from Japan, she will take Japanese—those who want to go, or those who have been ordered to leave—back with her. That is why the ship does not receive the usual happy greeting on Pier 8.

By shortly after nine o'clock, the ship is secured. Customs and immigration procedures begin. Immigration authorities are concerned with the proper papers for entry of the passengers, and the customs men handle clearance of any items purchased overseas. Secretly mixed in with them on this day, however, are other government men on a very different mission. They are agents of the Federal Bureau of Investigation (FBI) and members of Army Intelligence (G-2).

This newly arrived ship is of particular interest to them, because of the possibility that the Japanese government may try to "insert" a spy into the islands on this last visit. They watch closely and listen, as passports are examined and baggage is checked. They are performing their roles as counterintelligence agents, opposing the efforts of enemy spies.

After some hours, the *Taiyo Maru* is cleared. No documents or articles that would link her to intelligence activities are discovered; the passenger and crew lists seem to be in good order. So the authorities depart, and with them the suspicious FBI and G-2 agents.

But as these officials leave Pier 8, at least four Japanese on board the liner breathe sighs of relief. They appear on the crew list as members of the steward's department—those men of a ship's crew who act as waiters and food handlers and broom wielders and bed makers. Actually, the four men are officers of the Imperial Japanese Navy.

Two of them are submarine experts. The other two—the leaders of the quartet, Lieutenant Commander Suguru Suzuki and Lieutenant Commander Toshihide Maejima—are experts in air operations and in surface ship operations.

They have good reason to be relieved. For this voyage they are spies, and the *Taiyo Maru* has been a spy ship. So for all of them, the voyage from Japan has been tense. They have spent endless hours just looking out to sea and scanning the bleak skies.

Others in the crew have wondered why this four-some has been so interested in the skies and sea. In fact, almost everyone aboard the *Taiyo Maru* has been puzzled over her route to Oahu. She took the lonely northern passage between Midway Island and the icy Aleutians, one that frequently encounters heavy weather at this time of year. It was a very unusual course for a passenger ship to follow.

Suzuki and Maejima know why! The Japanese Navy ordered the *Taiyo Maru* to sail that northerly route. The four stewards were under orders to watch for ships and aircraft on this desolate sea path to Honolulu. Now they can report to Tokyo that they did not see a single vessel, not even a far-ranging fisherman; not once did they spot an aircraft in the gray, scudding skies.

To them, and to naval operations planners in Japan, including Admiral Isoroku Yamamoto, commander-in-chief of the Combined Fleet of the Imperial Japanese Navy, this is good news indeed.

Yamamoto is planning to attack Pearl Harbor and may well sail his ships along the stormy northern route.

The next morning, November 2, is warm, pleasant, and sun-patched as the crew of the *Taiyo Maru* debark for a shore visit. One of the first to go down the gangway is "Steward" Suzuki. He takes a taxi from Pier 8 to the Japanese consulate on Nuuanu Avenue, a short ride. Five buildings are enclosed in this compound, and in one resides the Honorable Nagao Kita, the consul general. A veteran diplomat, and a man who also knows quite a bit about sensitive intelligence work, Kita has been alerted from Tokyo by cable that he will be paid a visit by one of the "stewards" from the *Taiyo Maru*.

He can only guess as to the exact purpose of Suzuki's morning call, but considering recent requests for information from Tokyo and a previous visit by one of Japan's top naval intelligence operators, it is hardly a difficult guess. The visit has something to do with Pearl Harbor, and the great United States naval base.

The two men talk awhile, and then Suzuki hands Kita a tiny piece of rice paper. On it, in meticulous Japanese script, are ninety-seven questions about the naval base and other military installations on the island of Oahu.

The naval base at Pearl Harbor is headquarters

and home for two thirds of the 102 major fighting ships of the United States Pacific Fleet. Together with the Atlantic Fleet, composed of 114 major fighting ships, the vessels represent America's sea defense force.

Japanese naval experts well know that Pearl Harbor is the key to American sea power in the Pacific. Here the ships are provided with fuel and ammunition and are repaired. Pearl Harbor provides a base from which to conduct training exercises. Should the Americans lose this vital facility, they might not be able to defend their interests in the Pacific.

Also on Oahu are the big American Army Air Corps fields, Hickam and Wheeler; the Navy seaplane base at Kaneohe; the Marine Corps air station at Ewa; and another Navy field on Ford Island. Army troops are scattered throughout. Oahu is, in many ways, an island fortress in the middle of the Pacific.

The questions about it must be answered immediately. Soon Commander Suzuki leaves Kita's office and returns to the ship at Pier 8.

Kita then summons a young man named "Tadashi Morimura." He is listed in U.S. State Department records and in immigration records under that name, with his occupation as "apprentice consul." But Morimura has far more in common with Commander Suzuki than he does with Nagao Kita. His true name is Takeo Yoshikawa, and his rank in the Imperial Navy is ensign.

Since March, Yoshikawa has been extremely busy, but not with consular affairs. He, too, is a spy, and he has been collecting information on the American Navy, Army, and Marine Corps. Twenty-eight years of age, possessed of a ready smile, taller and heavier than most Japanese, Yoshikawa has made friends quickly. They range from waitresses and schoolteachers to members of the Japanese community. He is seldom around the consulate, and spends much time roaming over Oahu. Occasionally he visits the other islands.

He often goes sightseeing, and he has even flown over Pearl Harbor. Sometimes he talks to sailors and soldiers, but he is always careful not to ask too many questions. About the most daring thing he has done is to use his small camera on the plane ride over the naval base.

Most of Yoshikawa's activities, but not his aerial camera work, are known to American counterintelligence agents. They are considered normal and routine, part of the usual consular work. Every diplomatic outpost in any country gathers information, including military data.

Although the FBI and Army intelligence experts estimate that Nagao Kita has many part-time "agents" in his huge staff of assistants, spread out around all the islands, they do not suspect young "Morimura," the engaging apprentice consul. Even the other members of Kita's staff at the compound do not know that he is a spy. To them, he is a brash upstart and not very bright.

He is much wiser than he looks or acts. He has watched the warships parade in and out of Pearl Harbor, noting names and types, arrival and departure times. He has been most interested in the battleships and in the huge aircraft carriers *Enterprise* and *Lexington*. So he is well prepared to answer the questions submitted by Suzuki.

He goes over the list with Kita, and easily the most important question is: "What day would most of the ships be in Pearl Harbor?" His answer is quick and definite. A Sunday! Any Sunday!

From his months of patient observation, Ensign Yoshikawa knows that the ships of the Pacific Fleet usually steam back to port for the weekends after training exercises off the island. Sunday is always a religious day of rest for the Americans. There is something else about Sunday! Many of the off-duty officers and chiefs will be ashore. None of the ships will be fully manned.

Yoshikawa manages to answer most of the questions on the crumpled piece of rice paper, not really aware that he is helping to seal the fate of two nations on Nuuanu Avenue this balmy November day.

In the leisure of the afternoon, Consul General Kita is driven from the compound to Pier 8. He, too, has little real knowledge of the momentous decisions that are being made in Tokyo. At the moment he is just a courier, carrying out instructions. Kita boards the *Taiyo Maru* with an official-looking package under his arm. The ship is being watched by American intelligence agents, but it is not unusual for the consul general to visit his nation's vessels while they are in port, especially one like the chartered liner. Many legitimate matters of business require attention.

Kita locates Commanders Suzuki and Maejima, and they go into a room well away from prying eyes and ears. The door is locked. Then Kita opens his package, and the contents are spread out. They include maps of Pearl Harbor and of the military airfields, as well as sketches and aerial photographs. The documents, of course, represent the patient work of "Vice-Consul Morimura," otherwise known in the Imperial Navy as Ensign Yoshikawa.

By nightfall Suzuki and Maejima have accomplished most of their assigned mission. But the *Taiyo Maru* will be in port for two more days before she sets sail again for Japan. So they spend part of each day ashore and pick up other information. It is quite easy, as Yoshikawa learned before them. Fine souvenir picture postcard sets are available

in the shops, the kinds of sets that sailors often send home to girl friends and relatives. They contain photographic reproductions of some of the largest ships in the Pacific Fleet. On one postcard, there is an exceptional view of Battleship Row, the mooring area by Ford Island where the big capital ships tie up on weekends.

Suzuki, the aviator, is particularly delighted with the photograph. It is quite the best aerial view of Pearl Harbor that he's ever seen. It will delight the operations planners in Japan, too, should they decide to go ahead with the air raid they are mapping out. Reproductions of this view might also be excellent for taping to the instrument panels of the aircraft.

In late afternoon of November 5, the Royal Hawaiian Band strikes up on Pier 8. The *Taiyo Maru* is preparing to depart, and strains of "Aloha Oe," that happy and yet sad song, echo along the waterfront.

But not until after dark, about 7:30 P.M., does the Japanese liner finally slip away and stand out to sea, with 448 returning passengers.

For the four "stewards," especially Commanders Suzuki and Maejima, the voyage has been highly successful.

THE PURPLE MACHINE

2

Across an expanse of ocean and across a continent on this same day, this lazy day by the sands of Waikiki, a top-secret machine known only as "Purple" is clacking away in Washington, D.C.

Purple is a "code breaker." It consists of what appear to be two separate teletype machines, looking somewhat like the usual "wire" machines that are found in every newspaper office. Purple "breaks" coded diplomatic messages from Japan, making them readable and understandable once they have been translated. To use another term, it deciphers them, unscrambling the words that make up the secret code.

Intelligence and spying activities between nations are not a one-way street. While Yoshikawa and the men on the *Taiyo Maru* carry out their mission for Japan, Purple is at work for the United States and against Japan. Most nations, as a matter of security, relay all their important messages by code. Most, also, make an effort to break the codes of other nations and become privileged to the information.

Purple, after many months of brilliant work by cryptology (or code) experts, finally succeeded in breaking the Japanese diplomatic code in August 1940, and since that time the United States has had an "ear" in all the secret diplomatic messages transmitted between Tokyo and her officials stationed in America. Powerful listening posts, manned by expert radio operators, are spotted around the country and out on Pacific islands. They "listen" to the Japanese transmissions around the clock. The entire secret operation which involves Purple is designated "Magic."

Some of these messages, over the past months, have been rather alarming. Japan, incredibly, seems to be readying for war which goes beyond her moves in China.

President Franklin D. Roosevelt, Secretary of State Cordell Hull, Secretary of War Henry Stimson, and Secretary of the Navy Frank Knox know of the Magic operation and have access to the messages for the purpose of reading them. They cannot keep possession of them, not even file copies, for fear that unauthorized persons may see them. To trained eyes, the mere sight of the messages would reveal that the United States had broken the Japanese code.

Some of the top-ranking military officers, such as Army Chief of Staff General George C. Marshall and Chief of Naval Operations Admiral Harold Stark, are also aware of Purple's output. But Purple is of such a highly secret nature that few besides these key officials have any knowledge of the machine's existence and what it does. The military leaders in Hawaii, Admiral Husband Kimmel and Lieutenant General Walter Short, have never heard of it, nor do they realize that the United States is following every diplomatic maneuver that Japan makes.

Yet Admiral Thomas Hart, U.S. Asiatic Fleet Commander in Manila, and the British government in London both have Purple machines. Some United States officials think that both Manila and London need to know of the Japanese intentions.

Several of these closely guarded machines exist in Washington and they are administered by U.S. Navy Intelligence and by the U.S. Army's G-2. After the messages are decoded and translated, they are carried to the White House, the State Department, and other privileged offices in locked leather pouches. The security chain is the tightest in the entire government.

However, long before these now-crucial days of

early November 1941, President Roosevelt has thought about the possibility of conflict with the small, but very strong, Asian nation. As long ago as 1933, he mentioned it to Harry Hopkins, his long-time friend and confidant, in private conversation. Then, much later, in January 1941, Roosevelt wrote to the American ambassador in Tokyo, Joseph C. Grew:

> I believe that the fundamental proposition is that we must recognize that the hostilities in Europe, in Africa, and in Asia are all parts of a single world conflict. We must, consequently, recognize that our interests are menaced both in Europe, and in the Far East. . . .

Six days later, Grew wrote to the State Department:

> A member of the embassy was told by my Peruvian colleague that from many quarters, including a Japanese one, he had heard that a surprise attack on Pearl Harbor was planned by the Japanese military forces, in case of "trouble" between Japan and the United States; that the attack would involve the use of all Japanese military forces. . . .

But as the year ebbs out, the people of the mainland—the United States proper—as well as those of Hawaii, still think of Japan as a strange, backward place, so very far away that the country cannot be considered an enemy. If war does come to America, it will certainly be with that old enemy Germany.

To most people, Japan is a place whose inhabitants make cheap toys and have large front teeth and bad eyesight. They can't pronounce l's, and they say "prease" instead of "please." It is a silly, funny place, with kimonos and paper houses, where the people copy articles of merchandise made in the United States or England, and always take off their wooden clogs before entering a home.

Only a few civilians, and not even many military personnel, know that Japan has a larger and more modern Navy than does the United States; swift, new aircraft carriers; and, in some instances, superior planes and superior pilots. In reality, then, for a long time, "quaint" Japan, with its brooding inferiority complex, has been one of the most misunderstood nations on earth.

Being misunderstood, and underrated militarily, she is, at this point, very dangerous.

Many things have occurred since Japan moved troops into Manchuria in 1931—the result of an incident which Japan herself provoked. In 1937 Japan unleashed her armies for full-scale war with China, attacking at Marco Polo bridge, ten miles west of Peiping, the Chinese capital. That same year, she bombed and sank the United States gunboat *Panay* in Chinese waters.

But these events have been largely ignored by most Americans. A vast segment of the population wants to keep America isolated from troubles in the Far East or in Europe. It does not want war with either Japan or Germany. Even if England is conquered, it wants to remain aloof.

Yet, in the face of this political opposition, President Roosevelt has paved the way to supply England with munitions and old destroyers. He would like to do even more to help defend the British.

The Far East is another matter. It truly seems so remote to most Americans that they have tended to "look the other way" despite the *Panay* incident, other gunnings of United States naval craft, and the murder and harassment of American missionaries.

Then, there is the promise that President Roosevelt made during the election campaign of 1940. He assured Americans that he would not commit their sons to fight in foreign lands.

Yet more and more it looks as if he will have to break this promise, give even more assistance to England, and eventually "slide" into war with Hitler's Germany. But plainly, America is not equipped, nor in the political frame of mind, to fight both Germany and Japan. So the Far East remains a secondary threat.

However, as a secondary threat, Japan in 1941 controls vast territories within China and has its bases firmly established in French Indochina (an area that today includes the countries of Cambodia, Laos, and Vietnam). She is the most powerful nation in all Asia, and is on the march throughout Asia.

Bulging with people spread over her four main islands of Honshu, Kyushu, Shikoku, and Hokkaido, and dozens of smaller islands, Japan does need raw materials for her industry. She possesses relatively few within her own boundaries. These can be gained from China, from French-dominated Indochina, and from the oil-and-rubber-rich Netherlands East Indies (Indonesia). Holland's colonial empire includes Java, Sumatra, and part of New Guinea.

Japan also has its eyes on Malaya, Burma, the big island of Borneo, and even the Philippines.

But more than just a conquest of land and gain of raw materials drives Japan. The Japanese see themselves as leaders of all Asia, spreading influence both politically and militarily. They also resent "white" domination of land and economy in East Asia—domination by the British, French, and Dutch. They resent America's trade policies and her friendship with China.

These resentments were clearly evident even in

1938, when Prince Fumimaro Konoye, the prime minister, announced the concept of a "New Order" in East Asia, one in which Japan would lead the way not only in military and political affairs, but also in economic and cultural activities. The old slogan *Hakko Ichiu,* or "bringing the eight corners of the world under one roof," has been renewed. The majority of both the political and military leaders advocate expansion, and they find the majority of the Japanese people support this policy. When millions of people are crammed together on small islands, it is relatively easy to convince them they need more land.

The leaders also appeal to the ancient and overwhelming Japanese national pride, and the peoples' firm belief in their destiny. The leaders claim they can bring great and lasting prosperity to all Asia. The citizens of Japan listen and agree.

There is a peace party in Japan, and it might grow in strength, but the foreign powers, particularly the United States and Great Britain, do not seem inclined to give it much recognition or support.

Foreign observers feel that Japan's greatest desire is to be a major power, *the* major power in Asia. It does not matter that most of the people of Asia prefer to rule themselves, whether they be Chinese, Malayans, or Javanese. The Japanese, foreign observers say, now think they know what is best for all Asians.

There is something else! Underneath, and largely unsaid, but perhaps even more compelling than politics, is the *samurai* spirit, the spirit of the warrior.

Japan is now being blindly guided by the ancient ways of the *samurai,* the ways of the old warlords.

With England battling for its life in the air and on the seas against Germany; France and Holland already crushed by the German armies and Air

Midway

Hawaiian Islands

Wake

Marshall Islands

Gilbert Islands

The Pacific in 1941

Force, only one power stands in the warlords' way in the Far East and Pacific—the United States.

Since 1937 it has become increasingly clear that this is the only power that might block Japan's intention to extend the empire from China and Korea across the South China Sea to Malaya, Thailand (Siam), and even the Philippine Islands, where America has military bases.

Clearly, the United States cannot remain forever aloof and idle while Japan conquers China, the possessions of Holland in the East Indies, French Indochina, and British possessions. The United States is friendly to all four nations. More than that, Japan's military expansion poses a direct threat to the Philippines, islands protected by the United States. It is quite evident by now that Japan wants the Philippines as part of her "prosperity sphere."

Indirectly, Japan also threatens such United States mid-Pacific possessions as Midway, Guam, and Wake islands. All three have defense significance to the United States. Marines are stationed on Wake, and the island is a refueling stop for Pan-American clippers, the big amphibious flying boats, on their way to the Orient. Guam has been a naval refueling stop for years. Midway is the last defensive outpost before Hawaii.

Japan has bases in the Marshall Islands, the Gilberts, the Carolines, and the Marianas—possessions she gained after World War I. Guam, for instance, is less than a hundred miles from Saipan, a heavily fortified Japanese base in the Marianas. Wake is not too far from Japan's base of Kwajalein, in the Marshalls. So the United States has interests to protect beyond her commitments to allies.

Japan's leaders know that the "New Order" in Asia and the dreams of *Hakko Ichiu* cannot succeed unless the United States stands aside, or is defeated in battle.

Thus far, the United States has not used the force of its Navy in the Pacific or in Chinese waters. It has been increasing its military strength in the Philippines, and there are other signs that the nation is planning to face Japan squarely.

Up to this time, America has used only political weapons. It stopped the sale of scrap-iron to Japan, necessary to the war effort in China, in September 1940. It banned the sale of oil to Japan the same year. Without oil, Japan's war machine cannot long operate. In July 1941, with England as partner, America "froze" all Japan's assets in the United States, making it impossible for her to carry on any further trade with private businesses in the States and in England. The measures were all designed to force Japan to stop her warring in the Far East.

Of course America has also demanded that Japan cease fighting with China, withdraw from Indochina, and pursue a peaceful course in the Far East.

So, in these fall months of 1941, all but diplomatic relations between the United States and Japan have been severed. The two nations are still "talking" on high levels, but every other contact between them has been broken. They are enemies, but not yet at war.

Meanwhile, Japan has made treaties with Nazi Germany and Italy, as partners in the European Axis, and even a neutrality pact with Soviet Russia, who is now at war with Germany. On the other hand, America is firmly allied with Germany's foe, England.

So the sides are sharply drawn up, politically if not militarily—Germany, Italy, and Japan against England and the United States. America, at this point, well knows its enemies.

Yet few of Japan's leaders, except some high-ranking Army officers, want open war with the United States. They would like to achieve their objectives without it. Navy leaders, too, are generally against war. The highly regarded Admiral Yamamoto, who has served in America and is aware of its industrial might, spoke out earlier against such a move. In fact, so outspoken was Yamamoto that it was feared he would be assassinated by Army officers.

Once he made a talk at Japan's naval academy, telling the young officer candidates:

Most people think the Americans love luxury, and that their culture is shallow and meaningless. It is a mistake to regard them as luxury-loving and weak. I have lived among them, and I can tell you they are a people full of the spirit of justice, fight, and adventure. What is more, their thinking is very advanced and scientific. Lindbergh's solo crossing of the Atlantic is the sort of valiant act typical of them—a typical American adventure, based on science. Do not forget, American industry is much more developed than ours. And unlike us, they have all the oil they want. Japan cannot beat America. Therefore, she should not even think of fighting America.

Words like these enraged many Army officers, even though they knew that Yamamoto, having studied at Harvard and having been a naval attaché in Washington, was qualified to speak them.

Army influence, the *samurai* spirit, has grown steadily since 1937. Since this midsummer of 1941 General Hideki Tojo, the minister of war, has been one of the most powerful men in all Japan. Nicknamed "Kamisori," or "Razor Blade," Tojo seldom hides the fact that he believes war with America is inevitable.

Japan's Emperor, Hirohito, is a peaceful man, but by tradition rules Japan as a spiritual rather than a political leader. He does not want war with any nation, and while he is consulted and expresses his thoughts, he leaves the final decisions to his political leaders, who are more in touch with the global situation. Most of the time he is removed and aloof from the world, even from his own people, living behind the walls, moats, and manicured green gardens of the Imperial Palace in Tokyo.

Japan's prime minister until recently, Prince Konoye, was equally weak. He resigned his position in October rather than face the opposition of the Army. He is fearful of going to war with America. The new prime minister is none other than Kamisori, the tough, relentless "Razor Blade," General Hideki Tojo. He still holds his old post of war minister, and now is also the political leader as prime minister. It is a frightening combination of power, and without question he controls Japan.

Now there are feverish day and night meetings in Tokyo. The participants decide to submit still more proposals and demands to the American government. If the demands are not met, then Japan's military forces will be ready to begin operations in early December.

These demands, known as Proposal A, include United States acceptance of Japanese Army units remaining in North China, Mongolia, and Hainan for a "necessary period" and acceptance by the United States of a trade policy for China and throughout the Pacific that would remove all economic bans and restrictions on Japan. In addition, Tojo wants the United States to persuade China's leader, Generalissimo Chiang Kai-shek, to make peace with Japan.

The demands are harsh, and ask that the United States, in effect, sanction Japan's occupation of large areas of China and force Chiang Kai-shek to lay down his arms.

There is little reason to believe that America will accept Proposal A, and at almost the same time, since the military must plan ahead of political and diplomatic discussions, Admiral Yamamoto issues a secret operations order: "In the east, the American fleet will be destroyed. The American lines of operation and supply to the Orient will be cut. Enemy forces will be intercepted and annihilated. Victories will exploit the enemy's will to fight."

Despite his continued opposition to attacking the United States, Yamamoto is carrying out his orders as commander-in-chief of the Navy and as a professional military man. In fact it is Yamamoto who has conceived the plan to attack Pearl Harbor. Quite a while before this month of November, he said to Prime Minister Konoye, "If I am told to fight, regardless of the consequence, I will run wild for six months, or a year, but have no confidence for the second or third years . . . ."

Now, having ordered the destruction of the American fleet, Yamamoto issues still another order from his flagship, *Nagato,* directing the naval task force that has been selected to attack Pearl Harbor to assemble in Tankan Bay, also known as Hittokappu, in the Kuriles, a thousand miles north of Hokkaido, Japan's northernmost island.

Tankan Bay is an ideal place for the assembling of a secret battle fleet. Only a few fishermen live along its rugged shores. Snow-covered, the region is often hooded in mist.

Yamamoto, known far and wide in the Japanese Navy as an excellent bridge player and a winning gambler, is about to gamble in another game, one with very high stakes. He orders Vice-Admiral Chuichi Nagumo, the man who will command the fleet, to have his ships at Tankan Bay by November 22 for refueling and on standby for orders.

The date of the attack on Pearl Harbor has been set for Sunday, December 7, which will be Monday, December 8, in Japan.

Ensign Yoshikawa's advice for a Sunday raid has been accepted by Yamamoto and his Navy staff. Actually, Yamamoto had already decided on a Sunday raid but wanted affirmation.

Staggering and daring, certainly, the Pearl Harbor blow is but a part of an even larger plan. Almost simultaneously the Japanese will strike the Philippines, Malaya, Hong Kong, and Thailand. Then they will advance to the Netherlands East Indies, and finally occupy Burma. Their goal, within months, is to have troops along the border of India.

They plan to smash quickly the United States bases on Guam and Wake, later to take Midway.

Viewed on paper, in geographical outline alone, it is a staggering plan of conquest, and the bombs destined to fall at Pearl Harbor will echo throughout Asia.

THE SUBMARINES SAIL

3

By now, the end of the first week in November, Vice-Admiral Nagumo's strike force of the 1st Air Fleet is being readied for the long voyage.

His floating airfields, the carriers—the launching platforms for his aircraft—are his own flagship, *Akagi,* and the ships *Kaga, Soryu, Hiryu, Zuikaku,* and *Shokaku.*

The aircraft carriers will sail as a group—a task force—and to protect them from surface attack and provide antiaircraft defense, Nagumo will have the battleships *Hiei* and *Kirishima;* two cruisers, *Tone* and *Chikuma;* and nine modern, fast destroyers.

The destroyers, especially, will need more fuel for the trip, so oil tankers will accompany the task force to refuel it at sea, a hazardous undertaking when waves pile up. As an added precaution, the ships will carry extra fuel drums, and already those drums are being stacked up in Tankan Bay for transfer to the task force.

American ships are usually named for people, battles, states, cities, sometimes rivers; submarines often take their names from fish. But it is typically Japanese that *Akagi* means "Red Castle," *Kaga* means "Increased Joy," and *Zuikaku* means "Happy Crane." One of the destroyers was named *Kasumi,* which means "Mist of Flowers." But, of course, a *samurai* was also a poet and wrote charming verse on *shoji,* paper screens, before plunging his sword into an enemy.

The man assigned the key role in the formulation of Admiral Yamamoto's plans to strike Pearl Harbor is Commander Minoru Genda, a rather small, wiry man with bright, burning eyes, a crack pilot as well as a strategist. The plans were drawn up after much study, and a mock attack was even played out on a huge board at the Naval War College in Tokyo.

Genda has supervised the selection and the training of the pilots. They have been practicing since September, not realizing in the early weeks the mission that was ahead of them. They have "bombed" targets at Kagoshima Bay, on the island of Kyushu, and have made low-level torpedo runs, with torpedoes that were designed specifically for use in the shallow waters of Pearl Harbor. Not until the first week in October did the pilots learn of the daring plan to smash the United States fleet.

Now, Genda barely sleeps at all while he goes over and over the plans to destroy Admiral Kimmel's ships, and reduce America to a state of helplessness in the Pacific. On paper Genda has 432 planes available on the six carriers. Of this number, 353 have been designated for the attack missions. The others will be held either in reserve or for patrolling over the task force after the strike aircraft are launched.

The attacking force of aircraft, to be sent off the carriers in two waves, will include 103 Nakajima torpedo bombers, loaded with sixteen-inch converted naval shells. These planes will fly at a high level and drop their explosives on the ships or airfields below. There will be another 40 of the same type of aircraft with the shallow-water torpedoes slung beneath. They will come in low and release the deadly "tin fish" at the battleships and carriers. There will be 131 Aichi-99 dive-bombers, and finally 79 Mitsubishi-A6M2 fighter aircraft to engage United States fighter planes and also strafe ground installations with machine-gun fire.

Genda has been principally responsible for the selection of Lieutenant Commander Mitsuo Fuchida, an old friend, and like Genda, a fine and daring pilot, to lead the first strike wave.

So, all the elements are on paper, the pilots are trained, the orders have been issued for assembly! No nation has ever begun a war by an attack from aircraft carriers, and the fleet is indeed a formidable one that Vice-Admiral Nagumo, a stocky, balding officer, will command.

But beneath his brusque attitude, and behind the hard, cold eyes and sporty mustache, Nagumo is worried. Once the force sails, he is responsible for both fighting it and protecting it. He is not the gambler that Yamamoto is! The nightmare of being discovered prior to his attack, and losing his carriers, is never too far out of his mind.

There is also uneasiness in Washington, a feeling of uncertainty, but it is not of quite the same nature. On November 7, exactly thirty days before the attack date chosen by Yamamoto, President Roosevelt sits with his cabinet, asking for the latest information on the Japanese situation. He also asks for advice.

The distinguished, white-haired gentleman from Tennessee, Secretary of State Cordell Hull, soft-spoken but as tough as the hickory trees from his native state, says bluntly that the situation is serious, that Japan might attack at any time. But all present take this advice as meaning "attack" in the far reaches of the Pacific, perhaps bases in Malaya, or even the Philippines. Not Hawaii! In 1941, four thousand miles is a great distance.

It would take considerable imagination to arrive at the island of Oahu as a place the enemy would strike, simply because of its distance from Japan, and the key members of Roosevelt's cabinet are not particularly imaginative. Both Hull and Secretary of War Henry Stimson are aging, and ailing. Roosevelt himself, partially crippled from infantile paralysis, is not in the best of health.

This same chill night along the Potomac, Japan's ambassador to the United States, tall and scholarly Admiral Kichisaburo Nomura, calls on Hull to present his government's new Proposal A for peace in the Pacific. Hull, informed by Purple's decoded messages, already knows the terms that Nomura will present. But he pretends, of course, that he is reading Proposal A for the first time.

He does not reject the proposal, neither does he offer encouragement that the United States will accept it. He is simply polite and attentive, hinting to Nomura that Japan can find ways to become Asia's "moral" leader without being aggressive and occupying countries.

Then, at Nomura's request, Hull arranges a meeting with the President so that the ambassador can personally present his government's request to the American chief of state. This meeting takes place on November 10 at the White House, and Roosevelt's answer to Nomura is firm: *Japan can prove its desire for peace in Asia by beginning to move its troops out of China and Indochina.*

Hull, present at the meeting between Nomura and Roosevelt, notes the look of dismay spreading over Nomura's face. The Japanese ambassador knows that Tokyo will not listen to such advice, that Prime Minister Tojo will flatly reject it. By late afternoon of November 10, Proposal A, never a hopeful means to peace, is a useless document.

In fact, all of Nomura's sincere efforts are about to become quite useless. The admiral has no way of knowing it as he leaves the White House in dejection, but already eleven of Japan's submarines are moving toward Hawaii. They slipped out of the big naval base at Yokosuka the day before, and are now advancing to the north on a great-circle course to pass between Midway Island and the Aleutians, almost the same route plied by the *Taiyo Maru.*

Another nine sailed earlier. Five more will depart, these last carrying a particularly sinister weapon in the form of midget submarines manned by volunteers who have little hopes of returning to the Land of The Rising Sun.

For some time Nomura has been disheartened and has asked to be relieved of his post. A naval officer by training, and not a diplomat, Nomura has also requested help in the tense negotiations with Washington. In a few days another Japanese envoy arrives to take up residency at the embassy. His name is Saburo Kurusu, and he is a veteran and skilled career diplomat. But in appearance and manner, he is almost the opposite of lanky, friendly Admiral Nomura. To Cordell Hull, Kurusu immediately seems deceitful. Hull does not trust him at all, and eventually some in official Washington are to suspect that Kurusu knew well in advance of the plan to strike Pearl Harbor.

The subs have sailed, and in light of that, Kurusu's knowledge of Tokyo's final move is of little importance. If, by any chance, Nomura and Kurusu are successful in further negotiations, the submarines will be recalled, and the task force, not yet at Tankan Bay, will steam back to peaceful anchorages in the Inland Sea.

In Hawaii there is definite reflection of the anxiety in Washington, but it is far from causing an alert, or placing military units on a war footing. The Army commander, General Short, is much more concerned about the possibility of sabotage than he is about armed attack. He is worried that some of the more than 150,000 people of Japanese descent living in the islands may be more loyal to Tokyo than to their adopted land.

So Short has gone about stationing more guards at various installations and huddling his aircraft together at such fields as Hickam, Wheeler, and Bellows. He does this so that sentries can patrol with greater ease, and be on guard to prevent sabotage in case of war elsewhere in the Pacific.

Admiral Kimmel, a tall Kentuckian, a "spit and polish" officer, does not share General Short's fears of sabotage by Japanese living in Hawaii. He recognizes the dangers, but as commander-in-chief of all naval forces in the Pacific, he is more worried about hostile actions far away. For instance, Admiral Thomas C. Hart's Asiatic Fleet, a small and rather feeble force based in Manila, could be endangered.

On November 7 Kimmel's superior in Washington, Admiral Stark, wrote, "Things seem to be moving steadily toward a crisis in the Pacific. Just when it will break, no one can tell." Kimmel had received other such letters from Stark, beginning in April, but none contained a specific warning.

However, by now Kimmel has stationed submarines off Wake and Midway islands, the mid-Pacific bases, as sentinels, and in position to attack an approaching fleet. He has added more Marines to the small garrisons on Wake and Johnston islands, and he has placed certain vessels in United States west-coast ports on a twelve-hour sailing notice in case of a sudden outbreak of hostilities.

Yet he has not appeared to be particularly worried about immediate surprise attack on his ships at Pearl Harbor, ships that he can see daily from his commander-in-chief's (CINCPAC) office at the submarine base.

However, the officer he has relieved, Admiral James Richardson, openly viewed Pearl Harbor as a "mousetrap." Because of this, he pleaded with Washington to shift the main units of the fleet back to ports on the west coast of the United States. (Until the spring of 1940, the fleet had been based in California.)

The decision to base it permanently at Pearl Harbor was made by President Roosevelt, who believes it will act as a deterrent to Japanese aggression. Japan, naturally, views the decision as another sign of hostility by the Americans.

Richardson's open opposition to berthing the big ships at Pearl Harbor annoyed the President, and Roosevelt replaced him with Kimmel early in 1941.

So the battleships, ships that are still considered the strongest elements of the fleet by many—but not by aviation personnel—have their home in this harbor which Richardson likened to a mousetrap.

Of course there are also aircraft carriers, cruisers,

destroyers, and submarines, along with supporting vessels such as repair ships, oilers, supply freighters, tugs, and small craft. At times the "in-ship board," a type of bulletin board, of the 14th Naval District, also headquartered at Pearl Harbor, indicates more than a hundred vessels at docks, moorings, and anchorages.

The battleships are the largest of the surface vessels, with guns capable of hurling tons of shells at an enemy, barrels projecting from their main turrets like fat telephone poles. The cruisers are smaller, often faster, versions of the battleships. The destroyers, still smaller, fire not only guns but torpedoes, and are used to escort the larger vessels as well as fight off enemy submarines. The carriers, of course, operate fighter and bomber aircraft from their flight decks.

The ships often sail in task forces, units composed of all types of combatant ships. Essentially, task forces are "floating gun platforms," and their basic mission is to destroy an enemy fleet.

Kimmel and Short both face the same problem: too few men, and much obsolete equipment. Short's soldiers are drilling with World War I weapons, and Kimmel does not have enough patrol aircraft to maintain a far-ranging search of the waters off Hawaii. Both the Army and the Navy have suffered from a lack of funds, and only within the last two

years has there been an effort to rebuild the military defenses of the nation.

Perhaps even worse than the shortage of equipment—as old and worn as it is—worse than the lack of adequate manpower, is the lack of proper intelligence information from Washington. Headquarters for each of the military intelligence services are in the nation's capital, and they act as collection stations for information. Experts in Washington analyze the information received from various sources around the world, and then supposedly channel back pertinent data to field commanders.

However, by nature and by training, intelligence

personnel usually cloak their functions in heavy secrecy. Sometimes the secrecy is so jealously guarded that persons who need to know vital information, simply to make wise decisions, find out that the information is forbidden to them. Even President Roosevelt was taken off the Magic distribution list for a period because it was feared there were information leaks in the White House.

Both Kimmel and Short are unknowingly caught in this web of supersecrecy, because in mid-November they are still denied the knowledge of Purple and Magic. And Purple, especially with the arrival of Kurusu, is working overtime to decode the many messages from Tokyo, and from Washington to Tokyo.

On November 13, Admiral Nomura cables Foreign Minister Shigenori Togo in Tokyo to tell him that if Japan presses on with the "southward venture," the movement toward Malaya and Siam, the United States will surely join England in fighting her. Nomura suggests that Tokyo "be patient for one or two months in order to get a clear view of the world situation."

The next day, Purple decodes Togo's answer: The deadline for the solution of the negotiations has been set, and there will be no change. Press Washington for a favorable solution!

As the message is read in the State Department,

and eventually in the White House, there is little doubt in anyone's mind that a solid stalemate exists. As each day turns to night, the two nations have less to talk about, less room in which to make diplomatic moves.

Codes are curious, often chilling mixtures of words, and on November 19—as the Japanese submarines are progressing steadily across the Pacific, now trailed by the five U-boats with midget subs mounted in huge, waterproof steel tubes on their decks—another message from Tokyo to the Japanese embassy in Washington is intercepted. It is fed into Purple and comes out:

1. East wind, rain *(Higashi no kaze ame):* In case of Japanese and United States relations failing.
2. North wind, cloudy *(Kitanokaze kumori):* In case of Japanese and Soviet Russia relations failing.
3. West wind, cloudy *(Nishi no kaze hare):* In case of Japanese and British relations failing.

This "winds" signal is to be transmitted at the end of the regular Tokyo weather broadcast; each sentence is to be repeated twice. When it is heard, those in charge of embassies and consulates, in countries concerned, should immediately destroy all codes and other secret materials.

Read by personnel in both Navy Intelligence and

the Army's G-2, the message, soon to be known as the "Winds Execute Message," is interpreted by some to be a "war warning."

Plainly, it establishes procedures to be used in case of extreme international emergencies; plainly, it is an ominous message. Yet neither Admiral Kimmel nor General Short in Hawaii, nor Army commander General Douglas MacArthur in the Philippines, is notified of its existence. To tell them would probably mean revealing the existence of Purple and the fact that the Japanese code had been broken.

Five days later, Admiral Stark does send a top-secret dispatch to Admiral Kimmel, at Pearl Harbor, and to Admiral Hart, in Manila:

> Chances of a favorable outcome of negotiations with Japan very doubtful. This situation coupled with statements of Japanese government and movements of their naval and military forces indicate in our opinion that a surprise move in any direction including attack on Philippines or Guam is a possibility. Chief of Staff [General George C. Marshall] has seen this dispatch, concurs and requests action addresses to inform senior Army officers their areas. Utmost secrecy in order not to complicate an already tense situation or precipitate Japanese action.

Kimmel duly informs General Short, whose headquarters are at Fort Shafter, a serene old Army post not too far from Pearl Harbor, and Hart passes the message to General MacArthur in Manila.

But already time is running out. Nagumo's ships are at Tankan Bay. Singly, doubly, routinely, they have sailed from the Inland Sea, from Kure, and from Yokosuka. They are now shrouded by the mists of the Kuriles, and are busy loading fuel drums. American intelligence has no knowledge of their departure. Cleverly, ships that have been left behind have stepped up radio communications, sending a stream of false messages to be monitored by the unsuspecting American receiving sets. From all outward appearances, the carriers and the two battleships are still in the home waters of the Empire.

Of course, the other elements of Nagumo's strike force, the submarines, are well along their routes to Oahu. Even the five I-16 class midget sub carriers, proceeding via the direct route, under the very noses of Johnston and Wake islands, are having an easy, undetected voyage.

Because of radio silence, they cannot notify either Yamamoto or Nagumo, but they have seen no signs of American patrol activity. Certainly, they want to see none.

THE SHIPS SAIL

4

Beyond the Kurile Islands, which lie between Hokkaido—the northern island of Japan—and Soviet Russia's Kamchatka Peninsula, is the icy Bering Sea. The Kuriles face the cold Sea of Okhotsk. The region is icy and bleak, misty and snow-covered, the home of the seal and walrus.

Etorofu Island is the largest of the Kuriles, and Tankan Bay has the best deepwater anchorage. The rugged, practically uninhabitable land and the continuous bad weather make it a perfect hiding place for Nagumo's ships.

While shivering sailors transfer the drums of fuel oil to the ships, pilots on board the six carriers hold blackboard sessions and go to briefings. Engine mechanics work over the power plants of the Mitsubishi, the Aichi, and the Nakajima aircraft. Gunnery personnel go over and over the machine guns in the aircraft.

It is ironical that the superb Mitsubishi fighter plane was designed, some years previously, by an Englishman named Smith, who worked for the pioneer British firm of Sopwith. But the entire modern Japanese Navy has been patterned after the British fleet. Years before, England had lent its technology and knowhow to the rebuilding and modernizing of the Nippon naval forces. Even more ironical, perhaps, is the fact that much of Japan's latest equipment contains steel that came from the United States. Now, the very best ships and aircraft of the fleet are assembled here at Tankan Bay.

Aboard *Akagi,* the stern, sometimes irascible Vice-Admiral Nagumo frets and awaits developments. As hours tick away, Nagumo feels more and more that the mission is one he does not care to undertake. If he loses the precious carriers, Japan's ability to wage war may be ended. He will sail into the very heart of the United States Navy in the Pacific, and he has no absolute knowledge that they won't be waiting for him, and wipe him from the face of the ocean.

On November 25 Admiral Yamamoto issues the sailing orders, and they say, in part:

1. The task force . . . will leave Tankan Bay on the morning of November 26. . . .
2. Upon the opening of hostilities it will attack the

main force of the United States fleet in Hawaii
and deal it a mortal blow. The first air raid is
planned for the dawn of X-Day—exact date to
be given in a later order.
3. Upon completion of the air raid . . . the task
force will return to Japan.
4. Should negotiations with the United States
prove successful, the task force shall hold itself
in readiness forthwith to return and reassemble.

The negotiations are limping along, but both
nations are only playing a game, because on both
sides minds have already been made up.

Nomura now has a Proposal B and has already
given it to Secretary of State Cordell Hull. Once
again, because of Purple, Hull knows what is contained in the paper before Nomura hands it to him
on November 20.

Neither country will make armed advances in
Southeastern Asia and the Southern Pacific.

Each country will cooperate to receive commodi-
ties from the Netherlands East Indies.

Each country will mutually lift the bans on assets
that have been frozen, and resume trade relations.

The United States will provide Japan with the oil
it needs.

The United States will not interfere in China.

Proposal B is an insincere, almost insolent document, entirely unacceptable to Cordell Hull, and also to President Roosevelt. Yet diplomatic talk has to be kept alive, and a counterproposal is drafted, after Hull discusses the situation with the governments of Great Britain, Australia, The Netherlands, and China.

Time is the big factor! Each day that war does not start is a day toward the scant hope that it will not start at all. So Hull asks for more time to answer Proposal B. Nomura cannot grant this time on his own authority, and he sends a message to Tokyo.

The reply to the ambassador comes back swiftly, and the American radio monitors pluck it from the air waves for Purple to decode: ". . . if you can bring about the signing of pertinent notes, we will wait until November 29."

But the last sentence of this message to Nomura is a chilling one. "After that, things are automatically going to happen."

Nomura, it is said, does not know when or where these "things" might happen, but Kurusu, for one, seems to have no doubt that they "would" happen.

At noon on November 25, which is November 26 in Japan—Yamamoto's selected date for the departure of Nagumo's ships—Cordell Hull, joined by Secretary of War Stimson and Secretary of the

Navy Knox, goes to the White House, meeting Admiral Stark and General George Marshall before going in to see the President. Newsmen report that their "faces are grave, their moods somber."

The President says he thinks the United States may be attacked as soon as the next Monday (December 1). "The Japanese are notorious for making an attack without warning," Stimson later quotes Roosevelt as saying. The Japanese had attacked Russia in 1904 without any notification, and both Chinese incidents in 1931 and 1937, which were "attacks," though the Japanese preferred not to call them that, came without warning.

The meeting is adjourned, and the men go back to their respective offices with little to be heartened about. In fact, on returning to his office, Secretary Stimson is handed late intelligence information on the loading of Japanese troop and supply ships at Shanghai. Furthermore, the first elements of these Japanese naval forces are already steaming south. South is toward Malaya, Hong Kong, and Singapore.

Far away, at 6:00 A.M. this day, Tokyo time, with foggy darkness covering Etorofu Island, Nagumo's striking force heaves anchor, frigid water washing down the clanking chains. Then the ships vanish, like great gray ghosts, into the swirling mists. At dawn the few fishermen living on the hills behind Tankan Bay look out to their usual barren sea. That huge, mysterious fleet is gone!

The next day, at 5:00 P.M., Washington time, Cordell Hull gives Nomura and Kurusu the United States' answer to Japan's Proposal B. It is a long and detailed document, this Ten-Point Memorandum, and says, in so many words, that Japan must stop its aggression and begin a retreat in Asia.

The tiring, aging, white-maned Hull does not believe Japan will accept the proposal. To Prime Minister Tojo the memorandum means that Japan must turn back and give up what she has gained in China and Indochina. If nothing else, such a retreat would mean a great "loss of face," a loss of prestige, in Asia. This, Japan cannot accept.

Knowing the contents of the Ten-Point Memorandum and Hull's pessimistic feelings about it, the Army and Navy begin to send out messages to military commanders in the field. They are dated November 27. Those receiving copies include General MacArthur in the Philippines, Admiral Kimmel and General Short in Hawaii. The message begins: "This dispatch is to be considered a war warning . . . ." It forecasts that the Japanese might attack in the Philippines, the Thai, or Kra Peninsula, or possibly Borneo.

These are all places very remote from Hawaii.

With the exception of the Philippines, they are tied at this time to the British, the Dutch, or the French. Britain's big naval base, Singapore, is at the foot of Malaya, the peninsula extending out from Thailand. Even well-traveled military officers have to check their world maps to pinpoint Borneo, the island lying between the Java Sea and the South China Sea.

There are other messages tapping out on this tense day, including one to Short from Army G-2 warning him that sabotage can be expected. He replies that he is on the alert for sabotage and other subversive activities, and is coordinating his defenses with the Navy. His mind is still rather completely occupied with the dangers of internal disorders, certainly not with outside attack on his Army installations.

Short's reply to the War Department produces no reaction on the part of Secretary Stimson, General Marshall, and other high-ranking officers. They are satisfied that he has taken proper action.

In Japan, Prime Minister Tojo and his cabinet consider the Ten-Point Memorandum. Actually, they do not give it much thought. Tojo views it as an "insult." They also talk about the earnest cabled appeals of Nomura and Kurusu asking permission to continue their attempts to reach a peaceful accord.

Nomura and Kurusu receive an answer from Tokyo on November 28. Tojo informs them that the views of the Imperial government will be transmitted within a matter of days. Meanwhile, they must do the best they can, and not give the impression that negotiations with the United States have been broken off.

At the same time, Japan's news agency, Domei, releases a story for the press, giving the Japanese people the first official indications of the outcome of the negotiations. The Domei story calls the Ten-Point Memorandum an "ultimatum" and declares that "there is little hope of bridging the gap . . . ."

Tokyo's leading newspaper, *Asahi Shimbun,* comments, "A showdown has come . . . ."

For all practical purposes, negotiations have ended! Even the Emperor is helpless. On the next day, he summons his *Jushin,* the elder statesmen, to the Imperial Palace. They lunch and talk. Former Prime Minister Konoye hopes the two powers might continue their present relationship, deadlocked but not warring; former Prime Minister Mitumasa Yonai is afraid Japan may lose everything because of her fears of being strangled economically. The elder statesmen listen to an analysis of the situation written by Tojo, Foreign Minister Togo, and others.

Of those present at this meeting, only two Army

generals believe that war is the single course left for Japan.

In the afternoon the *Jushin* meets with the cabinet, expressing the same fears and doubts, but General Tojo is unmoved. To accept the economic sanctions imposed by America and England, he insists, is to die a slow death.

The *Jushin* does not know that Vice-Admiral Nagumo's fleet is on the high seas, steaming north and east. Neither does the Emperor, who has expressed his feelings poetically: ". . . why can't all men live in peace?"

However, another night is to spread across Japan before the final and formal decision to use military force is made. The Emperor agrees to a meeting of the Imperial Conference on December 1. This will be a last-minute review of the plans to open an Asiatic war front and strike the Hawaiian blow that will begin Japan's engagement in World War II. Germany has already agreed to support Japan and promises to declare war on the United States if Japan attacks.

These meetings, these far-reaching decisions, which will eventually touch almost every human being in all parts of the world, are not even dimly suspected by the people of San Francisco or Boston, by the residents of snowy Wyoming or warm Georgia.

Throughout America now, and on all the isles of Hawaii, Christmas decorations, those symbols of good tidings and goodwill to all men, are going up in shops and homes.

In Honolulu the strains of "The First Noel" and "Silent Night" float out with the liquid sounds of guitars.

There still is, in this part of the world, at this moment, peace on earth.

EXECUTE THE WINDS
MESSAGE

5

Ensign Yoshikawa has been busy. Each day he has observed the ships in Pearl Harbor, their arrivals and departures. On November 28, he reported to Consul Kita and then to Tokyo that the U.S.S. *Enterprise,* one of the three United States carriers in the Pacific, had gone to sea. Two battleships, *Oklahoma* and *Nevada,* along with a pair of cruisers and twelve destroyers, also cleared the harbor entrance that morning.

The *Enterprise,* with three heavy cruisers and nine destroyers, and with Vice-Admiral William F. "Bull" Halsey as task-force commander, was off to Wake Island to deliver a squadron of Marine fighters. The carrier *Lexington* is scheduled to leave in a few days to drop another squadron of Marine fighter planes on Midway Island. The only other "flat-top" in the Pacific is the U.S.S. *Saratoga,* now in San Diego waters for repairs. The old *Langley,* the Navy's first carrier, is in the Philippines, but it is being used as a seaplane tender and not an attack vessel.

More than any others, the aircraft carriers are the ships that Nagumo wants to destroy. He is an air admiral, and he well understands the power of air warfare. Like the air admirals of the American Navy, he no longer believes that battleships are the mainstays of a fleet.

So the movements of the flat-tops worry him. In fact, Yoshikawa's report on the departure of *Enterprise* causes alarm on the bridge of *Akagi* as the ship plunges steadily through fog and towering seas on the northern route. There is speculation as to where she is going, and why! It is something to think about as the ships proceed toward a refueling date, a final topping of the tanks before changing course and sweeping toward Hawaii.

Below decks, pilots and crewmen in the six carriers practice dummy bombing runs by dragging sheets beneath the aircraft. Targets have been drawn on the sheets.

Morale is high, and the pilots are anxious. The *samurai* spirit is very evident. Although America has been friendly for years, and most Japanese people have seemed to admire the United States, an almost ferocious hatred is being displayed now in the air groups. There is also an air of confidence.

Prime Minister Tojo convenes the Imperial Conference at 2:00 P.M. on the afternoon of December 1. The meeting has been called primarily for the benefit of the Emperor, because in most minds the decision to wage war has been made. There is no turning back as General Tojo explains the reasons why Japan must use military force. The Emperor sits quietly and does not utter a word. In the Japanese way, this silence permits those involved to claim that the Emperor has given the plans his "approval."

Only one major step must still be settled—the time that the United States will be notified of the opening of hostilities.

Both Admiral Osami Nagano, the Navy chief of staff, and his assistant, Vice-Admiral Seiichi Ito, had earlier demanded that the attack come as a complete surprise, without warning of any kind. They did not have too much regard for Yamamoto's daring plan, and like Vice-Admiral Nagumo they feared the loss of the entire task force if the enemy had time to gather a defense.

Yamamoto and Foreign Minister Togo disagreed with the Nagano position. Attack without warning was uncivilized. This was not the world of 1904, when the Russians had been taken by surprise. It was 1941 now, and there were rules for the conduct of war. Yamamoto insisted on some prior notification, an interval long enough for the United States to be aware that war was imminent, yet not long enough for the Americans to prepare themselves.

At this meeting of the Imperial Conference, Yamamoto's influence prevails. Hull will be notified of the termination of negotiations at 1:30 P.M., Washington time, December 7, thirty minutes before the first bombs are to fall.

But the diplomatic game continues, for Tojo stresses that the Americans must keep on believing that negotiations are still possible. This same day, Foreign Minister Togo terms the Ten-Point Memorandum "fantastic, unrealistic, and regrettable," for the benefit of Japanese newsmen, but issues a formal statement in softer words for Washington's benefit:

> The United States does not understand the real situation in East Asia. It is trying forcibly to apply to East Asiatic countries principles and rules not adapted to the actual situation in the world, and is thereby tending to obstruct the construction of the New Order. This is regrettable.

In the late afternoon Yamamoto receives his orders from Admiral Nagano: Japan, under the necessity of self-preservation, has reached a decision to declare war on the United States of America, the

British Empire, and The Netherlands. The commander-in-chief of the Combined Fleet shall at the start of the war direct an attack on the enemy fleet in the Hawaiian area and reduce it to impotency, using the 1st Air Fleet as the nucleus of the attack force.

The formal phrasing of the orders really boils down to one word: "attack." The next morning Yamamoto issues his own orders to Vice-Admiral Nagumo, using the decisive, prearranged code words *Niitaka Yama Nabore!* ("Climb Mount Niitaka!"), meaning, Attack Pearl Harbor, diplomacy has failed!

The wind is howling around Nagumo's strike force of twenty-seven ships as he receives this message. For almost four days he has been battered by the weather, and if the storm keeps up, his chances of refueling from the tankers are not good. Men have been washed overboard, and the little destroyers have taken a heavy beating from the rough seas. But the hooded skies and foul weather have also hidden him from observation.

Nagumo's first signal to his force after receiving the *Niitaka* message is to darken ships, and set Condition 2, a state of alert next to actual battle condition. The ships are blacked out and lookout watches are increased.

By day's end, the seas begin to calm and the task

force, steaming at thirteen knots, enters moderate to thick fog.

American intelligence experts are busy this first week in December attempting to monitor every kind of Japanese radio transmission. This is being done on the United States mainland, in Hawaii, in the Philippines, and at every other strategic wireless tracking outpost. Radio traffic is still heavy from Japan's Inland Sea as the ships remaining there tap out the false messages to cover Nagumo's absence.

But at Pearl Harbor, the Pacific Fleet's intelligence officer, Lieutenant Commander Edwin Layton, is mystified. He cannot "account" for two entire Japanese carrier divisions, comprised of four carriers and their supporting ships. No radio traffic has been received recently from the four carriers. In addition, the whereabouts of several Japanese battleships puzzles him.

Obviously the Japanese trick of increasing radio traffic in the Inland Sea has not been one hundred percent effective.

Layton informs Admiral Kimmel. The admiral reportedly replies, "Do you mean to say that they could be rounding Diamond Head now, and you wouldn't know about it?"

Various messages being intercepted in Hawaii at this time would probably be of great interest to Kimmel and Layton, who, however, do not know of their existence. Army Signal Corps operators pick up one from Tokyo to Consul General Kita:

> In view of the present situation, the presence in port of warships, airplane carriers, and cruisers is of utmost importance. Hereafter, to the best of your ability, let me know day by day. Wire me in each case whether or not there are any observation balloons above Pearl Harbor or if there are any indications that they will be sent up. Also advise me whether or not warships are provided with anti-mine nets. ["Anti-mine" nets, as the Japanese called

anti-torpedo nets, are made of steel, and extend out from the ship's hull to protect it from torpedo attack.]

The message is from Captain Kanji Ogawa, a key figure in Japanese naval intelligence and an expert on the American Navy, in particular. Ogawa had organized and administered the Japanese spy system in Hawaii.

On Wednesday, December 3, luck, an element highly respected by the Japanese, smiles on Vice-Admiral Chuichi Nagumo. The seas are calm enough to conduct refueling operations. Ships that need to be "topped off" soon have the wallowing big tankers by their sides, and fuel is pumped aboard. They steam steadily onward.

Just as the American operators are monitoring Japanese transmissions, radiomen in Nagumo's ships are listening to Hawaii around the clock, waiting for any indication of an alert, any warning that might tell them the task force has been discovered. Although no American aircraft have been sighted, nor any ships, the strike force could be viewed from the periscope of a patrolling submarine. Honolulu's KGU and KGMB come in clearly, but the stations broadcast only music, talk—nothing about an enemy fleet approaching.

In fact, Nagumo has luck that he doesn't even know about. A Japanese courier plane carrying Tojo's top-secret war plans to Canton has crashed in China's Waiyeung Mountains. But the Chinese Communist guerillas who find the plane cannot read, and they use the war plans to light their campfires.

On Thursday, December 4, there is a lot of movement in Pearl Harbor. U.S.S. *Lexington* sails for Midway Island with her cargo of Marine fighter planes. She is accompanied by three heavy cruisers and five destroyers. Carriers always have a screening force to protect them against surface or submarine action. *Lexington* is to conduct a combined search and battle problem to the south and west of Hawaii, after delivering the Marine fighters which will augment the weak Midway defenses.

Ensign Yoshikawa, ever present, always watching, duly records the departure of *Lexington* in a message to Tokyo, listing the number of ships that have sailed with her. This word is relayed to Nagumo. Now it is apparent that there may not be any carriers in Pearl Harbor on Sunday. It is disappointing news.

This same day, at least two, and perhaps more, naval radio operators hear a Tokyo news transmission that ends with *Higashi no kaze ame*—"East Wind, Rain." The phrase is repeated twice, the signal for all Japanese embassies or consulates in the United States or England to burn secret records and codes.

The intercepted message, later to achieve a certain fame in Congressional hearings as the "Winds Execute" message, is studied in Washington at the Navy Department. But those who see it supposedly come to the conclusion that it means attack in Manila, Hong Kong, Singapore, or the Dutch East Indies, or that it simply means that Japan will break off diplomatic relations.

Admiral Stark, Kimmel's superior, is one of those who reportedly sees this message, a stunning communication no matter what it means. Other members of his staff also see it, including Rear Admiral Richmond Kelly Turner, Stark's chief of war plans, yet Admiral Kimmel is not informed of it.

So another day, another night, will pass, and the calendar indicates that it is now Friday, December 5.

In Washington, Purple is clacking away with the latest intercept from Tokyo. It is an order from the Japanese Foreign Office instructing most of the members of the embassy to leave American soil within a few days. Before long, Nomura sends a cable back to Tokyo and Purple deciphers it: "Destruction of most of the embassy codes is completed."

Whatever attention these messages draw in military intelligence and in the State Department does not change the fact that in Hawaii, at least, Ensign Yoshikawa is taking direct action on his chores. He is aloft in a small chartered plane for a final look at the ships in port. It rained in the morning, and the day is chill, blustery, but the visibility is good. He studies the naval base.

Pearl Harbor is like a giant, irregular mushroom, with a rather narrow neck that leads out to sea. Ford Island, the naval air station, a base for both seaplanes and aircraft with conventional landing gear, sits in the middle of the harbor. Along both sides of Ford Island are ship moorings; on the south side is Battleship Row.

South, across the channel from Ford Island, is the naval station and the Navy Yard, with its drydocks, shops, and sheds. North of the naval station are the submarine piers and Kimmel's CINCPAC headquarters. Further south of the naval station is the Army Air Corps base, Hickam Field.

Ship anchorages are dotted all over the navalbase harbor, from West Loch, nearest the harbor entrance, back to the reaches of East Loch, usually a roosting ground for destroyers. There is also Middle Loch and Southeast Loch. The deepest water, of course, is around Ford Island, where the "heavies"—the battleships, the carriers—stay. Dredges

keep that water to a controlled depth of at least forty feet.

Yoshikawa has a good, long look at Pearl Harbor and Hickam Field, and then returns to earth again, going to the consulate compound on Nuuanu Avenue. Soon he begins to draft what will be one of his final messages from Honolulu. The message will inform Tokyo of the exact number of major combatant ships in port at day's end.

Meanwhile, a wax cylinder has been turning at the Honolulu FBI office, recording a conversation, in Japanese, between a person named Mori, in Honolulu, and a staff member of one of Tokyo's leading daily newspapers, *Yomiuri Shimbun*. For some time both the Army G-2 and the FBI have suspected that Dr. Motokazu Mori, a dentist, and his wife might be confidential agents.

Telephone lines to the Mori home on Wylie Street and to Dr. Mori's office on Nuuanu Avenue, not far from the consulate, have been tapped. The conversations are recorded on the wax cylinders. Mrs. Mori is supposedly a correspondent for *Yomiuri,* reporting on the activities of the large Japanese colony in Honolulu, but today's call, which her husband takes, seems rather strange.

Yomiuri asks, "Are airplanes flying daily?"

Mori answers, "Yes, lots of them fly around."

"Are they large planes?"

"Yes, they are quite big."

"Are they flying from morning till night?"

Many questions are asked, some that seem ridiculous. Others, though, inquire about searchlights and whether they are turned on when the planes fly at night; about the number of sailors around town; about the United States fleet; about the weather.

Then, completely baffling, "What kind of flowers are in bloom in Hawaii at present?"

Mori answers, "Presently the flowers in bloom are fewest out of the whole year. However, the hibiscus and the poinsettia are in bloom now."

After a few more questions, the conversation goes back to flowers again, and Mori says, "Japanese chrysanthemums are in full bloom here. . . ."

The wax cylinder keeps turning until the *Yomiuri* voice thanks Mori and signs off, "Best regards to your wife."

The questions are hardly of the type that are usually asked a newspaper correspondent over a long distance. Yet the two have talked not only about what might be military intelligence but about flowers and even herring roe and Japanese soy sauce. A very strange conversation!

The wax cylinder is removed but not translated until the following morning, a matter of routine.

THIS MEANS WAR

6

Saturday, December 6, in Washington, is only a partial day of work for many in the military establishment, even for the staffs of the intelligence and communications offices, although personnel are on duty around the clock. But no war alert, of any type, has been issued for either the Army or the Navy.

So the officers, sailors, soldiers, and civilians in the Navy Department, and in the War Department, housed in two old white buildings adjoining each other on Constitution Avenue, can look forward to going home at noon, or by four thirty, at the latest. Christmas shopping is much on the minds of most people.

Two officers are not so fortunate. They are Colonel Rufus Bratton, chief of the Far East section of G-2, Army Intelligence, and Lieutenant Commander Alvin Kramer, in the Far East section of the Office of Naval Intelligence. They are the counterparts of Japan's intelligence expert, Captain Ogawa, who is also very busy this day.

Both Bratton and Kramer have followed the Magic messages, as well as other monitored and decoded Japanese communications, for months. Lately, they have lived night and day with Magic.

Bratton has openly predicted war by November 30, but his superiors have not agreed with that estimate. Thus far, they have been proven right. November 30 has come and gone, and Bratton has been chided for his incorrect estimate. His "mistake" does not make him look like quite the expert that he is supposed to be. Also, his superiors won't be inclined to accept his judgment on future estimates.

Yet as this day dawns, Bratton is more than ever convinced that a Japanese attack is very near. He knows a lot about the Japanese and the way they think. He has had duty in Japan, and speaks the language fluently. He is the Army's chief expert on Nippon.

Tall, thin Alvin Kramer is also very much a "student" of the Japanese, and also speaks the language fluently. He, too, believes that war is only a matter of days, if not hours, away, but like Bratton has not been able to gather much support for his ideas from his superiors.

Even before Bratton and Kramer reach their offices this morning, a Navy radio-monitoring station on the west coast of the United States advises Washington that it has picked up a communication from Tokyo to Ambassadors Nomura and Kurusu. Soon the message is decoded and translated:

1. The Government has deliberated deeply on the American proposal of the 26th of November and as a result we have drawn up a memorandum for the United States contained in my separate message #902. (It will be transmitted in English, rather than Japanese.)

2. This separate message is a very long one. I will send it in fourteen parts and I imagine you will receive it tomorrow. However, I am not sure. The situation is extremely delicate, and when you receive it I want you to please keep it secret for the time being.

3. Concerning the time of presenting this memorandum to the United States, I will wire you in a separate message. However, I want you in the meantime to put it in nicely drafted form and make every preparation to present it to the Americans just as soon as you receive instructions.

This "pilot" message, telling Nomura and Kurusu how to handle the Fourteen-Part Message, which would break off diplomatic relations, is sent by Foreign Minister Togo.

Bratton correctly guesses that the Fourteen-Part Message to come will be of tremendous importance. He informs his superiors, Brigadier General Sherman Miles and Brigadier General Leonard Gerow, and then requests Navy help in handling it when it arrives because of its length.

At about the same time, a message from the Army's G-2 to General Short in Hawaii, telling him that the Japanese embassy in Washington is reported to have burned code books during the night, is supposed to have gone on the wires. But there is no record of this message reaching Short, and there is some confusion as to whether or not it was sent.

On the Navy side, the head of the security intelligence section of Naval Communications, Commander Laurence Safford, attempts to send a message to Admiral Kimmel instructing the Marine outpost on Wake Island to destroy all secret documents. Safford is worried that the documents might be captured if the Japanese land on Wake. But his superior, Rear Admiral Leigh Noyes, thinks that Safford is overestimating the danger; he also disagrees with the urgency of the matter. The message is then altered so that it will not cause alarm, and sent by the slowest method. Among the top officers, there seems to be definite resistance to the idea of Japan hitting the mid-Pacific islands, or closer still, Hawaii.

Such a message, not naming Wake Island specifically, does go out to Kimmel during the day on instructions from Admiral Stark. It gives Kimmel authorization to have his outlying bases destruct secret and confidential documents whenever Kimmel feels the need for it. But again, the communication conveys no sense of urgency.

In early afternoon, while awaiting copies of the Togo "pilot" message, the message which alerts Nomura to the long Fourteen-Part Message, Colonel Bratton leaves his War Department office in the Munitions building to go next door to the creaking Navy Department building for a chat with Commander Arthur McCollum, head of the Far East section for Navy Intelligence.

McCollum agrees with Bratton that war is likely within a few days, and they discuss Malaya and the Dutch East Indies area. Then Colonel Bratton wonders aloud about the possibility of an attack on Pearl Harbor. Commander McCollum almost scoffs at the suggestion. Besides, he says, the major units of the fleet are not at Pearl Harbor. He is positive they have sailed, or are about to sail.

Oddly enough, many of the top Navy officers also think the fleet has sailed. Probably some saw the departure reports on the *Enterprise* and *Lexington*. Two battleships had steamed out the same day as *Enterprise*, but had later returned. Whatever the impressions in Washington, the battlewagons, presumed the most powerful units of the fleet, are to be found at this moment on the south side of Ford Island.

There is much activity at the State Department and at the White House. Secretary of State Hull talks frequently during the late morning and early afternoon to both Secretary of the Navy Knox and Secretary of War Stimson. The calls result from a midmorning dispatch from the British Admiralty reporting two Japanese task forces moving slowly toward the Kra Peninsula, past Cambodia. A total of thirty-five troop transports have been sighted in these two groups.

Admiral Hart, in his headquarters at Manila, is already aware of this movement from his own sources.

Then, at the White House, on this sixth day of December, President Roosevelt makes a decision. In light of the events of the past week, he decides a direct appeal to Emperor Hirohito is the only course left open. The President knows that the Emperor has little control over the destiny of his country at this time, but there is always the chance that the saddened monarch in the Imperial Palace can somehow effect a miracle.

The second paragraph of Roosevelt's appeal be-

gins, "Only in situations of extraordinary importance to our two countries need I address your Ma-
jesty on matters of state. I feel I should now so
address you because of the deep and far-reaching
emergency which appears to be in formation . . . ."

Put in personal terms, the message is a friendly
one and uses the movements of Japanese ships toward Indochina as the basis of the dangers that
exist between the two nations, and the peoples of
Asia. But the cable to the Emperor, to be relayed
by Ambassador Grew, will not leave Washington
until about nine o'clock this evening, although it
was dictated to the President's secretary, Grace
Tully, in late afternoon.

Then, in Tokyo, the cable is held up many hours
by Japanese authorities, quite probably by design.

So even this final gesture by President Roosevelt
is caught in the traps of human error in Washington,
by its slowness of handling, and in the traps of in-
trigue in Tokyo. When Ambassador Grew finally
receives it, more than fifteen hours after it has been
dictated in the White House, the message is worth-
less.

The Fourteen-Part Message to Ambassadors Nomura and Kurusu begins flowing into Washington
after the noon hour, relayed from the Puget Sound
monitoring station and picked up also by another

monitor in nearby Maryland. But the Army has released its Purple operator for the day, and it falls on the Navy's machine to decode the message.

An inexperienced officer is on duty in the Navy section, and makes several mistakes in setting the proper "key" for Navy's Purple. The sensitive machine promptly breaks down, and not until late afternoon does another, more experienced officer, called back to duty, manage to get it in working order.

A little after 7:00 P.M. the thirteenth part clears the machine, and now the task is to type up the message neatly; there are more than three thousand words.

At 9:00 P.M., finally, six copies of the typed message are delivered to Colonel Bratton in the Munitions building. He has been waiting, and not exactly patiently, since noon. He is disturbed when he discovers that the fourteenth part has not been transmitted. Either the Navy monitors have missed it, or the Japanese have not sent it. Puzzled and frustrated, Bratton decides to go home after ordering an assistant to wait for part 14.

He attempts to reach his boss, General Sherman Miles, to tell him of the availability of the thirteen parts, but cannot locate him. He leaves a call for the general and then starts home, stopping by the State Department with his locked leather pouch containing a copy of the message. He delivers it to the duty officer at State with instructions that it is to be taken immediately to Cordell Hull at the Carlton Hotel.

At the Office of Naval Intelligence, a weary Commander Kramer gathers his six copies together. He informs McCollum and the ONI chief, Captain Theodore Wilkinson, of the general contents of the thirteen parts, and they agree the message should be delivered to the White House, and also to Secretary Knox, the sooner the better.

A bit after nine, Commander Kramer's wife pulls up to the Main Navy building on deserted Constitution Avenue, and she and her husband drive to the White House. The President has attended a dinner party given by his wife this evening, but leaves early, looking very "solemn."

Now, as Kramer arrives, the President is in the Oval Room with Harry Hopkins, who never seems to be too far away from Roosevelt and often earns his unofficial title of "second President."

Kramer hands his pouch to young Lieutenant Robert Schulz, on temporary duty as the assistant naval aide. The young officer takes it to the Oval Room and is admitted. He unlocks the pouch for the President, and remains standing nearby as Roosevelt reads other messages and then finally picks up the thirteen parts.

He reads the typed pages, passes them to Hopkins, who labors through them, and then Roosevelt comments, "This means war!" However, he does not summon his cabinet, nor does he relay his feelings of alarm to his military leaders. Perhaps he believes it means war within a week or a month, not hours.

The thirteen parts take up the many areas of disagreement between the two nations, stressing Japan's side of the issues, of course. The message refers to the Chinese war; to Japan's establishment of bases in Indochina; to American, British, and Dutch economic domination in Asia; and to past demands of the Japanese government.
Part 2 begins:

However, both the United States and Great Britain have resorted to every possible measure to assist the Chungking [Chiang Kai-shek's Chinese government] so as to obstruct the establishment of a general peace between Japan and China, interfering with Japan's constructive endeavors toward the stabilization of East Asia, exerting pressure on the Netherlands East Indies, or menacing French Indochina; they have attempted to frustrate Japan's aspiration to realize the ideal of common prosperity in cooperation with these regions.

Part 10 begins:

It is impossible not to reach the conclusion that the American government desires to maintain and strengthen, in collusion with Great Britain and other powers, its dominant position it has hitherto occupied not only in China but in other areas of East Asia.

Part 13 concludes that America, in collusion with Great Britain, Australia, The Netherlands, and China, and catering to Generalissimo Chiang Kai-shek, is ignoring Japan's position in Asia.

The thirteen parts leave little doubt as to Japan's grievances and leave little room for further peace negotiations.

Schulz recovers the documents, replaces them in the pouch, and leaves the Oval Room to return the pouch to Kramer, waiting in the White House basement.

The next stop for Kramer is the Wardman Park Hotel, residence of Secretary Knox. Knox is startled, too, by the message. He calls both Stimson and Cordell Hull to arrange a 10:00 A.M. meeting on Sunday morning, hopeful that the fourteenth part will have been transmitted by that time.

Kramer now crosses the Potomac River to Arlington, Virginia, where Captain Wilkinson lives. The Army's General Miles is a guest in the Wilkinson home this night, and they discuss the message. Both view it as a diplomatic and not a military threat; therefore they see no reason to awaken General Marshall at his quarters in Fort Myer, also on the Virginia side of the Potomac.

Wilkinson does reach Admiral Stark, and he, in turn, discusses the memorandum from Tokyo with President Roosevelt. Other high-ranking officers in the Navy are told of it, but each, on understanding that Admiral Stark knows of it, decides that the proper steps have been taken. Naturally, they go back to bed.

Among those in the Navy not informed this night is Admiral Husband Kimmel, commander-in-chief of the Pacific Fleet.

It is past midnight, already December 7 in Washington, when Commander Kramer and his wife go to their own home in Arlington. Extremely weary now, Kramer retires for the night. He goes to bed with the firm belief that Japan will "strike" within hours, probably at Singapore, plunging England into still another war.

LAST DAY OF PEACE: HONOLULU

7

A fire burns behind a building on Nuuanu Avenue in Honolulu this windy morning of December 6. The fire is of interest to an FBI observer since the building is one of five in the Japanese consulate compound. Consul Kita's bonfire is soon reported to General Short's intelligence staff, but unfortunately no one relays this information to the general himself.

The fire is the result, of course, of the "Winds Execute" message from Tokyo, and smoke is drifting up from Japanese government offices in numerous parts of the world. All secret records and codes are being burned.

Fires of a more intense nature are licking at the boilers of Vice-Admiral Nagumo's ships, now speeding toward position for the dawn launch tomorrow morning. The supply train of tankers has turned back, job done, and the Pearl Harbor Strike

Force is bending on twenty-six knots despite mounting seas.

At 8:00 A.M. Nagumo is handed a message from Tokyo, listing the ships present at Pearl Harbor as of December 5. Nagumo scans it, noting that the American aircraft carriers are still at sea. He wonders exactly where they are.

His orders from Yamamoto are to reverse course and flee if he is discovered before December 6, but it is now that date and there is no sign of discovery. The broadcasts from Honolulu continue to come in without interruption, with hour after hour of music and commercials, with no word of war preparations. Nor is there any indication that Ambassadors Nomura and Kurusu will score a last-minute diplomatic success, so Nagumo must press on.

If Nagumo were able to read the morning newspaper, the *Honolulu Advertiser,* he would learn from the headlines that America is probably going to reject Japan's reply on Indochina, and from a separate article, that the Japanese Navy is advancing toward the south, probably toward Indochina. The newspaper makes the gloomy prediction that the Nippon envoys have small chance of success with their negotiations. Yet there is nothing in the *Advertiser* to hint at falling bombs within another day.

In the afternoon Ensign Yoshikawa drafts another message for Tokyo: No barrage balloons can be seen around Pearl Harbor, and he does not think that anti-torpedo nets have been placed around the battleships. The big sausagelike balloons make it difficult for pilots to dive-bomb and strafe targets.

Tokyo promptly relays the message to Nagumo.

At about four o'clock, during the third quarter of the Shriners' football game between Willamette University and the University of Hawaii, the season's top sports event in Honolulu, Lieutenant Colonel George Bicknell, General Short's counterintelligence officer, receives a rather excited phone call from FBI agent Robert Shivers.

The "Mori" conversation of the previous day, that baffling dialogue between Dr. Motokazu Mori and Tokyo's *Yomiuri Shimbun,* has been transcribed from the wax recording cylinder and translated. Agent Shivers has the feeling that "something is going to happen."

Bicknell drives to the FBI office, at Merchant and Bishop streets in Honolulu, and reads the long list of questions and answers. He agrees immediately with Shivers that the conversation is ominous. It is certainly a strange conversation, with those references to aircraft, to searchlights! The blooming flowers? Could they be code words of some type?

Bicknell decides, in his role as a counterintelligence agent, that the conversation should be made known to General Short, and he calls Lieutenant Colonel Kendall Fielder, Short's G-2 representative. It is after five o'clock now, and Fielder explains that both he and the general have a social engagement tonight. But Bicknell insists the Tokyo conversation might be of utmost importance.

He goes immediately to General Short's quarters at Fort Shafter, fighting through the horn-honking traffic from the just-finished football game.

Short reads the transcription, but neither the general nor Colonel Fielder shares Bicknell's anxiety. They cannot figure out what the conversation means, and Fielder terms it "silly" from the western point of view. So the general ends this impromptu meeting at Fort Shafter by suggesting to Colonel Bicknell that perhaps his alarm is not really warranted. However, they will discuss it further in the morning. It is now 7:30 P.M.

Short and Fielder, with their wives, go on to the social engagement at Schofield Barracks, another Army installation, about twenty miles from Pearl Harbor, and Bicknell, understandably annoyed by their lack of interest, returns to his own home. He is unaware that the general has no knowledge of that earlier occurrence on Nuuanu Avenue, the burning of secret documents by Kita's staff.

At this moment, Admiral Kimmel is at the Hale-kulani Hotel on Waikiki Beach, near the world-famed Royal Hawaiian Hotel, a guest at a dinner party given by an Annapolis classmate. It has been a busy day for CINCPAC, ending about 3:00 P.M. after a staff meeting at Kimmel's submarine base headquarters.

The perplexing whereabouts of the Japanese carriers and the burning of the codes at the consulate were discussed, but attack, at least in Hawaii, was not even mentioned.

Four hundred miles away, in rolling seas that will make aircraft launching hazardous, and under heavy black clouds, all hands stand at attention in the ships of Vice-Admiral Nagumo. It is about nine o'clock. The loudspeakers ring out with a message from Admiral Yamamoto: "The rise and fall of the Empire depends upon this battle. Every man will do his utmost."

As the last words echo out on *Akagi,* a battle flag breaks from a halyard, flapping out in the strong wind. It is Admiral Heihachiro Togo's flag, the same flag that was run up on his command ship, *Mikasa,* thirty-six years earlier in the Straits of Tsushima just before his sweeping victory over the Russian fleet. The hoisting of it tonight is Yamamoto's idea.

Cheers roar from every ship of the strike force, and then another flag breaks from *Akagi's* top signal halyard: "Speed, twenty-six knots. Course south." The big task force wheels and begins driving across the whitecaps toward the dawn launch point 270 miles north of Oahu.

By 9:30 P.M. Admiral Kimmel, never a party man, is back home and in bed. General Short and Colonel Fielder have left the party at Schofield

Barracks and are headed back to Fort Shafter. Kimmel and Short have their regular Sunday golf game scheduled for the morning.

By 9:30 young Ensign Yoshikawa has sent his last message to Tokyo:

> The following ships were observed at anchor on the 6th: 9 battleships, 3 light cruisers, 3 submarines, 17 destroyers. In addition, there are 4 light cruisers and 2 destroyers lying at dock. It appears that no air reconnaissance is being conducted by the fleet air arm.

After the message is transmitted, Ensign Yoshikawa goes outside, guessing, but not knowing, that the attack is not too many hours away. Neither Kita nor Yoshikawa has been informed of the exact plans. Both realize they will be taken into custody after the bombs fall. The ensign looks at the haze of lights from Pearl Harbor. All seems peaceful; all seems quiet. Then he goes off to bed. It will be a restless night for Yoshikawa.

But it is definitely not bedtime for the majority of the off-duty personnel on Oahu. From Wheeler Field, with its planes parked neatly, wing tip to wing tip, patrolled by sleepy guards against sabotage, all the way past red-earthed sugarcane and pineapple fields to Pearl Harbor, the evening is a gay and noisy one.

Sailors on liberty and soldiers and marines with passes that permit leave this night jam downtown Honolulu, which glitters with the colored Yule lights. Movies, soon to let out, are packed. Taxis are doing a brisk business.

At the "O" clubs, the officers' clubs at the bases around the island, the bars are busy and dance bands play the hit songs of '41. That wishful song

"There'll Be Bluebirds over the White Cliffs of Dover"—there will be peace in England, somehow peace everywhere—is on every orchestra's request list.

At the Naval Receiving Station, in the new Bloch Recreation Center, there is even a contest going on between bands of the Pacific Fleet, a musical battle to see which ship's band is the best. It is a loud and happy time at the Bloch "rec" hall!

Silence does not begin to fall across the island until midnight when the bars close, and the sounds of "Good Night, Sweetheart," the romantic reminder that everyone should go home, drift up from a dozen places.

Offshore, only a few miles away, the scene is different. Long, threatening dark shapes of submarines are on the surface, and waiting.

WHAT DID "ONE O'CLOCK" MEAN?

8

There is a time difference between the mainland of the United States and its island possessions of Hawaii as the sun travels its east-to-west course, lighting up the continents and oceans on its way. At 7:00 A.M. in Washington, D.C., this crisp, clear Sunday morning, it is still deep night in Honolulu, with the Aloha Tower clock hands at 1:30 A.M., a difference of six and a half hours.

At seven o'clock, Colonel Bratton is en route to his office, as are Commander McCollum and Commander Kramer. Each man has spent a rather uneasy night with the knowledge that the crucial fourteenth part of the message from Tokyo is due to be sent to Nomura and Kurusu, or has already been sent. They reach their desks in the buildings on Constitution Avenue about the same time, 7:30 A.M.

Bratton needs to wait no longer. Already on his desk, decoded by Purple and Army personnel during the night, is the fourteenth part. The wording is not a particular surprise to the colonel:

> The Japanese government regrets to have to notify hereby the American government that in view of the attitude of the American government it cannot but consider that it is impossible to reach an agreement through further negotiation.

The other thirteen parts of the message, already received of course, mean little now. In this fourteenth part the Japanese have finally made their position clear, in plain, unmistakable words. The long diplomatic road has come to an abrupt end!

Bratton immediately routes copies to General Marshall's office, to Army G-2, and to the State Department. He also sends copies over to Commander McCollum in the Navy Department, and within minutes Commander Kramer departs for the White House with his locked leather pouch. Kramer has an extra copy for delivery to the State Department, an added measure to ensure that this important message will reach Cordell Hull.

While the fourteenth part is being delivered, another Tokyo intercept is fed into Purple:

> Will the ambassador [Nomura] please submit to the United States government (the secretary of

state) our reply to the United States at 1 P.M., on the 7th, your time.

After deciphering Part 14 of my 902 [the message number] . . . please destroy at once the remaining cipher machine and all machine codes. Dispose in a like manner the secret documents.

On reading it, Bratton gasps. ". . . 1 P.M., on the 7th, your time. . . ." It leaps out at him. It has to mean something. What time will that be in Manila? Two A.M., he figures quickly. What time in Hawaii? The answer is 7:30 A.M. Sunrise, or near it. *Hawaii!*

Bratton knows Japanese military history, and the examples of their previous attacks at sunrise. Attacks without warning! Or with a warning so subtle that the western mind does not comprehend it.

Bratton is frightened and goes immediately to General Marshall's office with the new intercept, but he is informed that the general is still in his residence at Fort Myer.

Bratton phones Fort Myer and is informed that General Marshall is out riding "somewhere along the Potomac." Often, on Sunday mornings, Marshall takes a canter on his favorite horse, King Story, with the dalmatian, Fleet, trotting faithfully behind.

In an urgent voice, Bratton tells Marshall's orderly that the general must be located; he must call Bratton immediately.

President Roosevelt is still in bed, at 10:00 A.M., when the fourteenth part is delivered to him by Captain John Beardall, his naval aide. He reads it, and reportedly his only comment is, "It looks like the Japanese are going to break off negotiations." He is also informed of the one o'clock meeting between Cordell Hull and the ambassadors.

Yet, strangely, he does not confer with Hull, Secretary of War Stimson, Secretary of the Navy Knox, or either General Marshall or Admiral Stark. Reportedly, he spends some part of the rest of the morning taking treatment for his sinus condition.

General Marshall returns to his home about 10:15 and calls Colonel Bratton about 10:25. He goes immediately to his office, reaching it sometime about 11:00 A.M.

A bit earlier, Commander Kramer returns from his rounds to find the "one o'clock" intercept. He, too, is alarmed and believes that the Japanese will "attack somewhere" at 1:00 P.M., but unlike Bratton, Kramer estimates the attack will come far out in the Pacific, perhaps in the Gulf of Siam, a blow against the British and Dutch.

He is not thinking of Pearl Harbor.

In Admiral Stark's office a conference takes place between the admiral, his top staff, and Commander

McCollum. They all agree there is something "significant" about the "one o'clock" message, and it looks for a moment as if Admiral Stark will place a telephone call to Admiral Kimmel in Honolulu, but then he decides against it.

In General Marshall's office another conference is under way, and Marshall, after reading the fourteen parts and aware of the last Purple decipher—the one o'clock delivery instruction—places a call to Admiral Stark. America's two top military leaders confer, and Marshall suggests an alert be sent to Hawaii, Panama, and the Philippines. But Stark thinks that enough warnings have already gone out.

However, General Marshall does draft a message:

> The Japanese are presenting at 1 P.M., Eastern Standard Time, today, what amounts to an ultimatum. Also, they are under orders to destroy their code machines immediately. Just what significance the hour set may have we do not know, but be on the alert accordingly.

This message is intended not only for Hawaii but for the Army commands on the west coast of the United States, as well as in Panama and the Philippine Islands. It is 11:50 A.M. (5:20 A.M. in Honolulu) when Marshall gives the message to Colonel Bratton for transmission.

So the Army, if not the Navy, is going to be put on war alert.

At the Signal Corps message center the duty officer, Colonel Edward French, checks the various methods of sending the message in order to determine which would be the quickest. For almost two hours this morning the War Department's radio circuit to the Pacific has been having static troubles.

French finally decides to send the message by commercial telegram. It will be relayed by RCA radio. Had he used the powerful Naval Radio Station at nearby Arlington, Virginia, the message would have reached Hawaii in minutes.

Over at the State Department, Secretaries Hull, Stimson, and Knox are holding their meeting, scheduled the previous night. They all feel that Japan is ready to attack, but they spend most of the time before lunch discussing what the United States might do if the Dutch and British are fired on.

So the morning passes.

General Marshall returns to his quarters at Fort Myer; Secretary Knox meets with Admirals Stark and Turner for lunch, and President Roosevelt has his lunch in the Oval Room at the White House, and looks forward to working on his stamp collection in the afternoon.

The war alert from General Marshall? It is on its way to Hawaii, but has been sent *routine* instead of *urgent*.

"DEPTH-BOMBED SUB"

9

Five dark shapes, long and low, are on the surface of the waters about eight miles off Pearl Harbor this chill, windy Sunday morning. They are the 1st Submarine Squadron, five of the undersea craft that sailed from Japan in November, and the time has come for their stealthy operation to begin.

At 1:00 A.M., Hawaii time, they slide beneath the chopping water, leaving only great boils and foam on the face of the ocean. No one sees them. In a few moments four of them release the midget submarines they have carried across the Pacific in big, watertight tubes on the decks.

In the fifth submarine, the I-24, the midget craft is having compass difficulty, and twenty-three-year-old Ensign Kazuo Sakamaki, its skipper, and his teammate, Petty Officer Inagaki, urge the mechanic to hurry repairs. They are anxious to join the attack.

Manned by volunteers, men willing to die for their country, the first of the so-called *kamikazes,* the midgets have orders to penetrate the harbor once the aerial attack is begun. They have been training for months for this single mission.

The little boats look like oversized torpedoes, with conning, or control, towers attached to them. Forty-one feet long, each sub carries two torpedoes and despite its small size can travel 175 miles on its storage batteries. So the eight miles to the harbor entrance is no distance at all for the midgets.

Since there is a steel antisubmarine net strung across the entrance to Pearl Harbor, anchored on both shores with a gate in the middle, the men plan to follow behind incoming American ships. They will hide in the churning wakes and sneak past the steel netting, then lie on the bottom of the harbor until the airplanes begin to bomb. Then they plan to surface and release their deadly torpedoes.

The plan is a startling, daring one, and even Admiral Yamamoto has serious doubts about it. But the spirit of the men and their willingness to go on this first of the *kamikaze* "suicide missions" sways his judgment.

With Ensign Sakamaki and Petty Officer Inagaki still struggling with the faulty gyrocompass on board their small U-boat, the other four midgets, floating free of their mother subs, set course for the entrance to Pearl Harbor, moving at five knots.

A bit later, Sakamaki—anointed with ceremonial perfume, wearing the *hashimaki,* the *samurai* headband, and clad in a leather jacket and a *fundoshi,* a scant piece of cloth like a pair of trunks, little more than a bikini bottom—gives up on the balky compass and passes the word that he is now ready to be launched.

Far to the east of the thin trails of bubbles on the ocean, there is other movement in the night. Twelve United States Army Air Corps B-17 bombers are droning through the skies en route to Hickam Field for refueling and a rest stop after a flight from the West Coast. Under the command of Major Truman Landon, the big four-engined bombers are headed for the Philippines to help General MacArthur's forces there.

It is a fourteen-hour flight from California for the big planes, long and tiring. They are flying individually instead of in formation, because formation flying requires more gas. Fuel is a very definite problem. To save weight, the planes have been stripped of all but essentials. Even their machine guns, protection against fighter-plane attacks, have been rendered useless with heavy coats of preservative grease.

In their communications compartments and the pilot wardroom, radios are tuned to Honolulu's station KGMB. The Army had requested that the station play music throughout the night to aid in guiding the B-17's to a safe landing at Hickam Field in the morning. They will "home" in on the KGMB broadcasts.

Ironically, of course, this same recorded music, mostly Hawaiian songs, is being heard on Nagumo's carriers. They are "homing," too.

The hour approaches 2:00 A.M. Although most of the Pearl Harbor Strike Force pilots try to sleep, it is a tense, restless night in the task force, and Vice-Admiral Nagumo, for one, does not leave the bridge of *Akagi*. He knows that he can be discovered at any moment by one of the twin-engined Navy PBY flying boats on patrol. His ships are making long tracks of phosphorescence in their wakes, easily spotted from aloft. Maybe an American destroyer or a submarine routinely snooping along will see the big force.

The uninterrupted music from Honolulu is calming, though. If the Americans were aware of his ships, the air would crackle with warnings, or the station would be ordered off the broadcast bands. But the normal programs play on, and it is now almost 4:00 A.M., time for the aircraft crews to be awakened for launch preparations.

In the background, from KGMB, come such soothing songs as "Sweet Leilani, Heavenly Flower . . ."

Chugging along outside Pearl Harbor is the small United States minesweeper *Condor*. The possibility always exists that an enemy submarine might come up and lay mines, floating or submerged explosives, around the harbor entrance. So the *Condor*, with a sister-ship, *Crossbill*, has the boring job of "sweeping" the waters with equipment that will catch or explode the planted mines.

Of late the men of *Condor* haven't even caught a fish, much less a mine, but at 3:42 A.M. by the bridge clock watch officer Ensign R. C. McCloy sights an unusual white wave off to his port side, the left side of the ship. The wave is moving, and less than a hundred yards away.

McCloy watches it and then requests his helmsman, the man at the wheel, to look through the binoculars. They decide it is a submerged submarine, and both know that submerged subs are not permitted around the harbor entrance. Any sub approaching Pearl Harbor must be on the surface, and all the sub skippers know this.

A few minutes later *Condor*'s blinker light flashes out a message to the nearby U.S.S. *Ward*, an old destroyer also on routine patrol off Pearl: "Sighted submerged submarine on westerly course, speed nine knots."

The *Ward*'s commanding officer, Lieutenant William Outerbridge, puts his ship on action alert by sending it to "general quarters," and for almost an hour a search of the area is conducted. But the midget submarine, probably sighting the *Condor*, has changed course and gone farther out to sea to await a better opportunity to move into the harbor entrance.

Lieutenant Outerbridge takes the *Ward* off alert and the ship continues its search, but in a more leisurely and routine way. Outerbridge eventually goes to his cot on the command-deck level, to be handy in case something else is sighted.

The sea plays many tricks on human eyes, and it is always very difficult to be certain that a deadly U-boat has been sighted. Whales, fish, floating logs, and even tin cans have been mistaken for the undersea marauders. A ship has often been called to general quarters, her guns manned—and the "sub periscope" has turned out to be a harmless branch of a tree. The *Condor* may have sighted a real sub or just another branch.

Meanwhile, the sea-gate to Pearl Harbor, the gate in the middle of the antisubmarine nets, has been opened. At a few minutes after five the *Crossbill* moves through, and just after five thirty the *Condor* calls it a night, ends her sweeping, and is logged as entering the harbor.

Traffic is scheduled to move out of the harbor soon, at daybreak, so it doesn't make sense to the sailors manning the booms to close the gates. Either opening or securing the booms takes ten minutes, usually.

The Japanese midget subs now have clear access to the naval base's waters if they are lucky enough to find an incoming ship and hug her wake, entering behind her.

In this black predawn, aboard Nagumo's carriers less than 250 miles from Pearl Harbor, the pilots are dressing. They bathed last night, and this morning some, like Ensign Sakamaki, dab special perfumes on their bodies. There is much ceremony. Even the breakfast is ceremonial. It is *sekihan*, rice boiled with tiny red beans, a dish eaten only on the highest and most solemn occasions.

The seas are still heavy; the carriers pitch and roll as they continue southward. Aircraft are already on the flight decks, and dotted over them are spurts of blue exhaust as mechanics warm up the engines. Two seaplanes have been launched from the heavy cruisers *Tone* and *Chikuma*. They are winging toward Pearl Harbor for a final reconnaissance of the American bases.

Breakfast finished, the pilots go to the briefing rooms of *Akagi, Kaga, Hiryu, Soryu, Zuikaku,* and *Shokaku*. Before them, on blackboards, is the latest information on the American fleet, as well as wind and weather data.

Vice-Admiral Nagumo comes down from *Akagi*'s bridge to the briefing room to give the pilots a pep talk, and then he speaks privately to the flight leader, Lieutenant Commander Fuchida. Grasping Fuchida's hand, the crusty flag officer tells him that he has every confidence the raid will be successful.

The pilots then drink ceremonial *sake,* the traditional Japanese rice wine, and pause a moment to pray before the small Shinto shrines that are on board each ship. There are cries of "banzai!"—the Japanese warrior chant—and then the pilots run to the flight deck, scrambling into their planes.

Fuchida's aircraft, a three-seat Nakajima-97 (Kate) with a bomb beneath, has red and yellow stripes on the tail. To avoid alerting the Americans he alone can use his radio once the planes are airborne; he will direct all the other pilots on the first wave until they get over target. He will give the final order to attack.

Ready to man his plane, Fuchida is stopped by the chief of the aircraft maintenance crew. He is handed a *hashimaki,* the same type of headband that Ensign Sakamaki is wearing in the midget sub. Wearing this headband means that the warrior is ready to die for his country. Tears in his eyes, Fuchida straps it on, and then climbs into his cockpit.

Every crew member not on duty below decks is now crowding the flight decks of the carriers. Al-

most every eye in the task force, above decks, is watching *Akagi,* waiting for the launch signals. A trail of steam arises from each flight deck, indicating the wind direction. It is east, and brisk, fine for launching, although the high seas cause the flattops to pitch, creating a hazard.

Flags are run up on *Akagi,* straightening out and popping in the wind. The formation swings around, heading the carriers directly into the stream of the wind. The ships settle down on the new course.

Now Vice-Admiral Nagumo's personal battle flag arises on *Akagi* to join the tatters of Admiral Togo's banner from the great Russian victory of 1904.

On the deck of the *Akagi* a green light makes a circle in the thinning darkness as the launch officer waves the first aircraft to takeoff. Chocks are pulled, and full throttle is pressed. The lead aircraft trembles with power as the brakes are released.

Cheers are drowned out by the thunder of Lieutenant Commander Itaya's Zero fighter plane as it charges down the deck, blue exhaust stabbing out from its manifold; the plane dips as its wheels leave the wooden planks. It seems to hover under the bow of the ship for a moment and then gains altitude, vanishing into the gray-black predawn.

Aboard the five other carriers, it is much the same—the fighters take off first to fly protection for the bombers and torpedo aircraft. Finally Fuchida's plane is launched from *Akagi* as a bright orange sun begins to peep above the horizon.

The aircraft join up in formation, and Fuchida, calling on all his twenty-five years of flying experience, leads them toward Pearl Harbor. The time is about 6:30 A.M., and it will take them more than an hour to arrive over target.

While the 1st Air Fleet is jockeying into formation to the north, the American naval supply ship *Antares* is arriving off Pearl Harbor after a trip to the South Pacific island of Palmyra. She is towing a barge, and going out to meet her from Pearl Har-

bor is the tug *Keosanqua,* the main reason why the antisubmarine gate has been left open.

The *Ward* is still prowling about, halfheartedly looking for that mysterious submarine the *Condor* reported. Then Seaman H. E. Raenbig, at the helm of the *Ward,* sees something very curious in the wake of the *Antares.*

It's a black object, in between the *Antares* and the barge she is towing. This object is also spotted by the pilot of a Navy patrol bomber circling overhead. To Raenbig, it looks like a submarine.

Lieutenant Outerbridge is awakened from his doze on the cot and takes a look himself. Only one look is needed. He orders the ship to general quarters. *No question about it, that is a sub out there.* He signals all engines full ahead.

In the Navy patrol plane above, Ensign William Tanner has an even better view of the U-boat. But he thinks the submarine is an American vessel in distress. He drops two smoke bombs on it, so rescuers will have an easier time spotting it.

Outerbridge isn't thinking about rescuing anything. He is planning to attack. The little sub that is following the *Antares* has its conning tower about two feet out of the water. It is not like any submarine Outerbridge has ever seen. The U.S. Navy does not have midget submarines!

"Commence firing," Outerbridge orders.

The first shot, at 6:45 A.M., which became the first shot of the war between Japan and America, zooms harmlessly over the midget sub. Gun Captain Russell Knapp's second shot smashes the sub's conning tower, and the little craft reels as the *Ward* steams past, banging against the hull of the destroyer.

Seconds later, four depth charges roll from the stern of the old four-stacker, sending geysers into the air, smashing the U-boat to the bottom.

Then the PBY patrol plane, seeing the action below, joins in, and the ocean erupts again!

The U-boat that was following the *Antares* is definitely sunk and destroyed, but now, on the *Ward,* and up in the Navy PBY, there is a lingering question: did the submarine belong to the Pacific fleet? Ensign Tanner is having second thoughts!

But Outerbridge, a veteran officer even though his rank is only lieutenant, has no doubts about what he has done. *He has carried out his orders.* He radios the 14th Naval District Headquarters at Pearl Harbor: "Depth-bombed sub operating in defensive sea area." The time is 6:51 A.M.

After a moment's consideration, Outerbridge decides to send an even stronger message: "Attacked, fired on, depth-bombed, and sunk, submarine operating in defensive sea area."

Now, at the 14th District headquarters, there should be no mistake as to what has happened off the harbor entrance.

ATTACK! ATTACK! ATTACK!

10

That "mysterious thing in the hills," the electronic device that caused some gossip back in November, is operating this morning. It is top secret, and is a British invention called radar. On mobile platforms, so that it can be moved from place to place, the device is an electronic "eye" that can look far out over the seas and into the sky.

There are five such radar stations spotted around the island, and when working, they can pick up an aircraft 150 miles away. The unit sends out a beam and when an object interrupts the beam a "blip," a small mark, appears on the glass tube or scope that is not unlike a television tube.

Telephone lines run directly from these mobile radar stations to the Combat Information Center at Fort Shafter. When an operator sees a "target," an incoming or outgoing aircraft or ship, on his radar scope, he immediately informs Fort Shafter and the target is plotted on boards. It is "tracked" as it moves along. A decision is made as to whether the aircraft or ship is "friendly" or "enemy." If it is thought to be the latter, an alert is issued.

The Opana mobile radar station, on a high ridge near Kahaku Point, on the north end of Oahu, is always manned each day between 4:00 and 7:00 A.M. General Short believes this period is the most likely time for an enemy to attack.

For almost three weeks Army Privates Joseph Lockard and George Elliott, hastily trained for radar operation but by no means experts on the amazing new apparatus, have had this lonely duty at Opana. They are there to spot aircraft and report them to Fort Shafter, but the job is looked on as training more than anything else. They have had no enemy to report.

This morning the two men awakened at a quarter to four, and had the radar warmed up and working by 4:00 A.M. sharp. Only now, at 6:45 A.M., do they see anything on the scope. They report several planes approaching from the northeast, more than a hundred miles out. (These are probably the reconnaissance seaplanes launched from *Tone* and *Chikuma.*)

But the duty officer in the Information Center at Fort Shafter, Lieutenant Kermit Tyler, makes nothing of them. In fact, Lockard and Elliott are advised to "secure" the set, to shut it down.

Fifteen minutes later the Information Center is practically deserted. Everyone except Tyler has gone off to breakfast. He still has one hour of duty left, and then the center will be closed down until tomorrow morning. Tyler is an Army Air Corps pilot, and this duty is simply additional training for him. It's rather boring, too.

Back at Opana, Lockard and Elliott are waiting for the breakfast truck to come rolling up their ridge, and to while away the time they decide to keep the radar set in operation. Elliott, who has the least experience, is at the dials when a large blip shows up on the scanner. It is so large that Lockard thinks the radar set must be out of order.

He sits down at the dials. No, the set seems to be working all right, although they've had constant trouble with it. Like any other new apparatus, especially a sensitive electronic gadget, it has "bugs." But the system is certainly working okay now. As Lockard reads off the distance, and direction, Elliott plots the blips.

The blips are 137 miles away, to the northeast, larger than any either Lockard or Elliott have ever seen on the scope. Dozens of planes!

At 7:06 an excited Private Elliott calls Fort

Shafter, getting through to Private McDonald, the switchboard operator. McDonald listens, scribbles down the information, and takes it to Lieutenant Tyler, who is waiting only for the clock hands to settle on 8:00 A.M.

Tyler is not at all disturbed by the large image on Opana's scope, and McDonald calls Lockard to tell him that the lieutenant isn't concerned.

The blips are bigger than ever, Lockard reports, and closing in rapidly. At 7:15 A.M. he estimates they are only ninety-two miles away.

Again, Private McDonald attempts to impress Lieutenant Tyler, and requests that he talk personally with Lockard. Tyler picks up the phone and listens to Lockard, but decides the planes must be friendly. He knows the Navy carriers are out on operation, and it is possible that some Army aircraft are arriving. KGMB has stayed on the air all night, usually an indication of an incoming overseas flight.

"Don't worry about it," Tyler finally tells Lockard.

But the breakfast truck still hasn't arrived, and the two young privates continue to watch the blips as they come ever closer.

By 7:39 A.M. they are twenty-two miles from the island of Oahu.

Lieutenant Outerbridge, on the U.S.S. *Ward,*

has sent his two messages off to the 14th Naval District Headquarters, but they were coded. It takes a few minutes to handle and decode them, so not until 7:12 A.M. does duty officer Lieutenant Commander Harold Kaminsky see the startling slips of paper. He calls Captain John Earle, chief of staff to Admiral Claude Bloch, who commands the naval district.

Now, almost thirty minutes have passed while Earle and Bloch confer on this report from Outerbridge. Both officers are surprised by it, to put it mildly. Depth-bombing a submarine almost on the edge of the harbor? Surprising, if not stunning news.

There have been a number of sub-sightings within the last few months, not many of them confirmed, and it isn't clear in the minds of either Earle or Bloch that Outerbridge actually *saw* the U-boat that he claims to have depth-charged, fired on, and sunk. They want positive confirmation, and so inform Commander Kaminsky.

It is 7:40 now, only one minute after Opana radar has established that the planes are twenty-two miles away, and the phone rings in the quarters of Admiral Kimmel, at Makalapa, a housing area across from Pearl Harbor on higher ground, affording a good view of Battleship Row.

Kimmel is told of the *Ward*'s action, cancels his golf date with General Short, and prepares to go to his headquarters at the sub base to investigate the details of the claimed sinking.

At about this moment, Lieutenant Commander Fuchida, leading his forty-eight Nakajima B5N1 high-level, or horizontal, bombers—each carrying a 1,600-pound armor-piercing converted naval shell—looks down through a hole in the clouds. He sees a long tumbling line of surf that pounds in along the north coast of Oahu. The navigation has been good. He is over Kahuku Point.

He couldn't ask for better weather. Even the ten-knot wind is from the north, aiding him. There are heavy clouds around the mountain peaks east and west of Pearl Harbor, but the weather report indicates only scattered clouds over Pearl Harbor itself. He has been listening to station KGMB, and in fact, only moments before has made a navigational change to home in on the broadcast beam.

Spread out in the skies around, below, and above him, is the strike force. To his right, and at a lower altitude, are Lieutenant Commander Murata and his forty Nakajima-97 (Kate) torpedo planes; to his left, the fifty-one Aichi dive-bombers, with 500-pound bombs, led by Lieutenant Commander Takahashi.

Above the bombers and torpedo planes, flying protection, watchful for any arising American air-

craft, are the forty-three Mitsubishi Zero (or Zeke) fighters, ready to respond to orders from Lieutenant Commander Itaya, who had the honor earlier this morning of being the first pilot off the *Akagi*.

They drum on through the broken clouds, no other aircraft in sight. Actually, a few civilian planes are aloft, but no Army aircraft are up, except the incoming flight from California, the B-17's commanded by Major Landon. No Marine planes have been airborne out of Ewa Field this morning, and the few Navy patrol bombers on duty are routinely scanning areas at various distances from Oahu.

Fuchida is still not certain that the Americans are truly asleep down there and have no knowledge of his presence in the skies. The scout planes from *Tone* and *Chikuma* whose job is to report on enemy air defense have been silent. Nonetheless, at about 7:40 it is time to make his decision, time to deploy his aircraft. There are two plans, one if "surprise is achieved," and the other if "surprise is lost."

Fuchida believes that surprise has been achieved, and he slides his cockpit canopy open. He fires a visual signal with a flare pistol—"One Black Dragon." It means the torpedo planes will go in first and hit the major ships; then his own horizontal bombers, and finally the dive-bombers, will attack. This was Genda's carefully planned tactic.

Commander Murata sees the "One Black Dragon" signal and starts his torpedo group down to a lower altitude; the dive-bombers begin a climb to 12,000 feet. Fuchida's own group will fly at 3,500 feet for the horizontal bomb runs. But the fighters, above them, do not seem to be responding to the signal. So Fuchida fires a second shot from the flare pistol.

Although Fuchida means simply to arouse Commander Itaya and his Zeros, the dive-bomber pilots take the signal to mean "Two Black Dragons," or "surprise is lost." Now, as the planes proceed along the coast in a southwesterly direction, there is confusion in the skies as both the dive-bombers and the torpedo bombers are headed for a simultaneous instead of a separate attack.

Some civilians, and undoubtedly some military personnel, see the aircraft in the sky along the coastline between Kahuku Point and Kaena Point, and while they wonder about the large numbers of them, they are not alarmed. The Army or Navy is exercising, they decide, although it's not usual for a Sunday. None of the planes are close enough to reveal the "red meatballs" on their fuselages.

At 7:49 A.M., when the formation, splitting up, is just about opposite Waialua Bay, Fuchida turns to his radio operator, Warrant Officer Mizuki, and orders the attack. Mizuki hits his Morse code key: "To . . . to . . . to!" Attack! Attack! Attack!

The torpedo bombers swing inland to fly parallel to the Waianae Range en route to the naval base; the fighters and dive-bombers turn sharply across the island to hit at Wheeler Field and then Kaneohe Naval Air Station.

Fuchida continues southeast with his level bombers, cutting across land by Kaena Point and flying on to orbit off Barber's Point to await his moment of attack.

There is still no sign of opposition from the ground, no fighter planes buzzing up from Wheeler or Ewa or Ford Island, no bursts of antiaircraft fire from hidden guns. Fuchida is amazed, and four minutes later he orders Mizuki to radio back to Vice-Admiral Nagumo, and the task force, 200 miles away—closer than had been originally planned—"Tora! Tora! Tora!" Tiger! Tiger! Tiger! It is the code transmission for "Complete Surprise Has Been Achieved."

Nagumo receives the news without visible emotion, but certainly there is great relief on all the carriers. Admiral Yamamoto, aboard his flagship, the *Nagato,* in Japan's Inland Sea, is notified. The *Nagato's* radio room, monitoring the bands, has also heard Fuchida's message.

Like Nagumo, Admiral Yamamoto displays no emotions but asks that the time of attack be carefully checked. Fuchida's signal means that other Japanese attacks throughout the Pacific and the Far East will begin. The message from Hawaii is earlier than had been planned. Clearly, Fuchida is ahead of schedule.

But at this hour of 7:53 A.M., the first bomb has yet to fall; the first bullets have not sprayed out of machine guns. The Japanese aircraft are roaring to their strike positions, their main targets being the battleships, Ford Island and the naval base, and Wheeler and Hickam fields. But aircraft will split off and hit other targets—Kaneohe Naval Air Station and the Marines at Ewa. Each pilot knows his primary targets.

On the American ships, it is nearing time for colors, the morning raising of the flag. There they sit, the might of the United States Navy in the Pacific. Battleship Row is occupied this morning by U.S.S. *California,* moored by herself at the head of the row; behind her, against a dock, is the fully loaded gasoline tanker *Neosho;* then more big ones, *Oklahoma* and *Maryland,* together; *West Virginia* and *Tennessee* side by side; *Arizona* moored inside the repair ship *Vestal;* finally, by herself at the end of the row, *Nevada.*

They are tied to concrete quays, huge pilings that are offshore from the banks of Ford Island.

Across the channel, almost directly opposite *California,* the cruiser *Helena* is tied inboard of the old *Oglala* at the naval station's dock. The battleship *Pennsylvania* and the destroyers *Cassin* and *Downes* are in the mammoth Navy Yard drydock. At dock in Southeast Loch, opposite the sub base, are the cruisers *New Orleans, San Francisco,* and *Honolulu.* Five subs are in port.

On the other side of Ford Island, four ships are tied to the deepwater mooring quays: the cruisers *Detroit* and *Raleigh;* the former battleship *Utah,*

Pearl Harbor, the morning of December 7, 1941

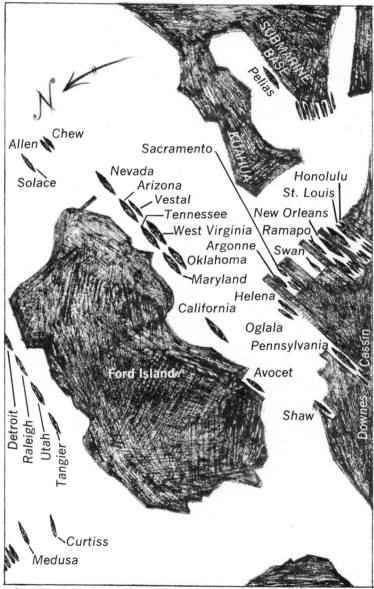

After *Pearl Harbor: Why, How, Fleet Salvage and Final Appraisal*, by Vice Admiral Homer N. Wallin. U.S. Government Printing Office, 1968.

now a target vessel; and the seaplane tender *Tangier*.

Spread out around the harbor, in Middle Loch and East Loch, and at other anchorages, are destroyers nested together and support ships.

More than ninety commissioned vessels are in the harbor, and all await this daily routine of colors. Then those personnel who are not on duty can relax. The next occasion of any kind is church call; after that, "chow down," which usually comes between eleven thirty and twelve o'clock.

Sundays are lazy and quiet on the ships of the fleet.

At approximately 7:54 A.M. Admiral Kimmel, still at his quarters in Makalapa, is getting off the phone with yet another perplexing report from the destroyer *Ward*. Now she's caught a sampan, a small fishing boat, with Japanese on it, in the defensive sea area.

At this minute of 7:54 A.M. General Short, his golf game with Admiral Kimmel having been cancelled, is at his quarters at Fort Shafter.

It is the last minute of peace.

THIS IS NO DRILL!

11

They are like maddened bees in the warm, early air, buzzing over Oahu, streaking between the billows of clouds in a half-dozen places. Some come through Kolekole Pass, a craggy, narrow V in a mountainous cliff of the Waianae Range, almost directly behind Wheeler Field and Schofield Barracks.

The lines of attack, swift arrows crossing the rich green fields, begin to split up again, fighters and some dive-bombers peeling off to descend on Wheeler and Schofield; dive-bombers driving ahead toward Kaneohe Naval Air Station, some splitting off again toward Pearl Harbor and Hickam Field.

Within minutes, attacks are being made on every major military air field on the island. Yamamoto's plan is to cripple the United States' ability to launch an air defense, and Genda's tactical plan, outlining the details, working from intelligence information, is to leave the parked aircraft as blazing wrecks.

At Ford Island Naval Air Station a single plane dives toward the seaplane ramp. A black object tumbles from it, and the earth shakes as the plane screams up skyward. On its side is a bright red "meatball." The time is 7:55 A.M.

Commander Logan Ramsey, on duty in the Ford operations office, has been busy directing additional aerial help to the *Ward* for submarine search. He hears and feels the jar of the explosion, and then sees the plane. He gasps, "It's a Jap!"

Commander Takahashi has his planes over Hickam Field, and they begin to peel off toward the runways where the Army aircraft are side by side in neat rows. General Short's exaggerated fears of sabotage, helped along no little by the directives from Washington, are about to blow up, almost in his face. There are booming explosions at Hickam, and black, oily smoke thrusts up into the sky.

General Short hears the explosions, but thinks the Navy must be having a battle practice. He goes outside his quarters at Fort Shafter, and does see smoke to the west. But it doesn't occur to him that the smoke is from bombing and strafing.

In these first seconds and moments of the attack, only two people on the soil of Oahu understand completely what is happening—Consul General Nagao Kita and Ensign Takeo Yoshikawa. Later Yoshikawa is to say that he had "strange feelings" when he heard the noise and saw the smoke.

At 7:56 enemy aircraft are sighted heading toward the northwest side of Ford Island, toward that line of ships headed by the seaplane tender *Tangier.* A few seconds pass, and then torpedoes slam into the *Raleigh* and *Utah.* This, too, is incredible! Most of the high-ranking officers in the U.S. Navy had thought the waters of Pearl Harbor were too shallow for torpedo attacks. Another myth, like the myth of distance, ends with a fiery roar.

Men aboard the ships on Battleship Row hear the explosions from the other side of the island and are baffled. Some see the aircraft, far away, but assume Army or Navy pilots are practicing combat tactics. Yet it is strange for a Sunday morning, always a rest day.

A single Kate dashes across Ford Island, unleashing its torpedo toward the naval station's docks and the cruiser *Helena,* tethered inside the aged minelayer *Oglala.* There is a red burst amidships on *Helena.* Time, 7:57 A.M.

Slowly for some, immediately for others, but in amazement for all, the men understand they are under enemy attack. It is no practice, no drill! At 7:58 A.M. Rear Admiral Patrick Bellinger, commanding the land-based air arm, issues the first signal to all

ships in the harbor: AIR RAID ON PEARL HARBOR! THIS IS NO DRILL!

Now, at 8:00 A.M., the breathtaking official CINCPAC confirmation message goes out to all naval commands around the world.

But the attack encompasses much more than

"Pearl Harbor." At Kaneohe, machine guns chatter as Val dive-bombers zoom in, spraying fire-producing tracer bullets, which can be visually *traced* through the air for more accuracy in bombing. In less than a minute, thirty-three of Kaneohe's patrol planes are afire. At Ewa Marine Corps Air Station, west of Pearl Harbor, forty-seven of Colonel Claude Larkin's forty-eight planes go up in flames and smoke as twenty-one Japanese raiders attack.

More of Murata's torpedo planes are after the big ships. They thunder in across Southeast Loch, low over the water, so low that their propellers churn whitecaps. They aim for the massive battlewagons moored at the concrete quays, the towering steel residents of Battleship Row.

On *Nevada* the band is playing the national anthem for morning colors. Musicians on the exposed afterdeck calmly keep blowing their horns, following the leader's baton, in a stunning demonstration of both shock and long training. Machine-gun bullets tack across the deck from a Kate that has already thrown its torpedo at *Arizona*. But not until the last note of "The Star-Spangled Banner" is played do the musicians run for cover.

General quarters, the call to arms, is sounding repeatedly on all the ships in Pearl Harbor. Frantic voices convince the men that the raid is real, not some drill by crazy pilots. Whining aircraft, ear-shattering explosions, and now the screams of wounded men are beginning to say more than the urgent voices on the loudspeakers.

Oklahoma is hit, then *West Virginia.* Two torpedoes smash into *Arizona.* The *California* is hit with a pair.

A monitoring radio operator at the Mare Island Naval Station in San Francisco has heard the first incredulous Pearl Harbor broadcast ordered by Rear Admiral Bellinger, meant only for ships in that area. He has relayed it to Naval Communications in Washington, and now an excited radioman calls Admiral Leigh Noyes, the top officer in communications.

Noyes, too, is stunned, but doesn't wait for confirmation, and runs to Admiral Stark's office. But the admiral has already gone for the day. Noyes now goes directly to Secretary Knox's office. Knox reads the message and blurts out, "My God, this can't be true! This must mean the Philippines." He thinks a mistake has been made.

Knox calls the White House and repeats the message to President Roosevelt. Later there will be different reports as to how the President reacted, but the most reliable one, from Harry Hopkins, will be that Roosevelt said he thought the news was "probably true."

Roosevelt phones Stimson first, and then at 2:05, just as Ambassadors Nomura and Kurusu are being ushered into the waiting room outside the secretary of state's office, he calls Cordell Hull. Roosevelt then makes other calls and dictates a statement for release to the press before resuming his lunch with Harry Hopkins.

Various accounts later on will indicate the President remained "cool" and "calm" throughout. Hopkins' diary will later reveal that the President seemed to be "thankful" that the "matter was out of his hands." The enemy had chosen to strike first, and now the United States could retaliate with a clear conscience. Also, the United States could now wage war against Germany and Italy. No longer would the nation be isolationist; no longer would Roosevelt have to keep his campaign promise of not sending American boys to fight on foreign soil.

At 2:20, Washington time, Hull requests Nomura and Kurusu to enter his office. He does not ask them to be seated, the usual polite gesture. He asks Nomura why he had been instructed to deliver the message at one o'clock. Of course, Hull already knows the answer: the time element—that didn't work— between the starting of the attack and the notification of a break in relations.

The Japanese ambassador begins to explain that there were difficulties in recording it, but Hull interrupts him in cold fury. He tells them that their Fourteen-Part Message is full of lies and distortions. Nomura starts to answer, but Hull simply waves them out of the room.

Not until they meet newspapermen in the corridor do they learn their country has attacked the United States.

Five minutes earlier the President's announcement of the attack has gone out to the news services, and at this moment America's radio stations are informing a shocked and stunned people. It is to be a moment that almost everyone over the age of six, at that time, is to remember for the rest of his life.

At first the announcement is met with disbelief. No one can believe that the "little brown people" from Asia have done this. Then it is met with anger.

In Tokyo it is December 8, of course, and the Japanese people are equally stunned when the Imperial Rescript, the message from the Emperor, is read:

> We, by grace of Heaven, Emperor of Japan, seated on the Throne of a line unbroken for ages eternal, enjoin upon ye, Our loyal and brave subjects:
> We hereby declare war on the United States of America, and the British Empire . . . .

Antiaircraft fire is finally reaching up into the

Hawaiian skies. It has taken about five minutes for the Americans to gather their senses and begin manning guns. Puffs of exploding shells start to dot the air. From ships and shore batteries, every available and undamaged gun is getting into action.

Nevada's mast-top machine guns probably down the first enemy aircraft. The plane splashes into the water astern, but its mission has already been completed. A torpedo arrows into the port bow of the battleship and explodes.

Oklahoma is hit again by a torpedo. Darkness settles in the spaces below decks throughout the ship. Her generators are off the line, and even the emergency lights have been blown out. Three more torpedoes slam into her port side, ripping it open to the oily waters of the harbor.

The *West Virginia* takes another, and then at 8:05 the *California* is hit from the water. Seconds later, she shudders from another torpedo impact.

The deadly torpedo plane runs, led by Murata

and Lieutenant Goto, are almost over, and Lieutenant Commander Fuchida now begins his phase of the attack with the high-level bombers. He sets a course toward *Nevada,* wreathed in smoke. Ackack—antiaircraft fire—bursts in the sky around the Kate bombers.

Aboard *Oklahoma, West Virginia,* and *California* water is pouring in. Many men—engine-room personnel, ammunition handlers—are below decks on the ships. They hear the rumbles from above and feel the hammerlike blows of concussion through the steel skin of the hulls. Acrid, choking smoke curls down through the passageways and vent systems. Gagging fumes sweep into the steel mazes, sectioned off with watertight doors.

West Virginia settles to the bottom, the first ship to sink.

Above, bombs are spilling from Fuchida's high-level planes. One sailor describes them as "black snowflakes." The little repair ship *Vestal,* tied outside *Arizona,* takes a bomb that rips out part of her bottom. It was aimed at *Arizona,* and then two bombs find that ship.

Oklahoma is mortally wounded. Slowly now, the proud battleship rolls over. It is such a slow roll that men topside walk along the belly of the hull and find themselves standing on her wet bottom. Her mast and superstructure push into the mud. Some men jump into the water, which is covered with oil and ablaze in some places. *Oklahoma* is gone at about 8:08.

Inside her, men scream and panic as water begins to fill her compartments, leaving only pockets of air. They swim and claw in a world of darkness, with decks up where overheads are supposed to be. Trapped inside her hull, they have no sense of direction. More than four hundred men are trapped inside *Oklahoma*.

ARIZONA DIES

12

At about 8:11 A.M. there is a searing flash on *Arizona* as one of Fuchida's high-level bombers makes a lucky hit, blowing up the ship's forward powder magazines and forward boilers. Fuchida's own plane rocks in the concussion as a ball of flame and smoke shoots up into the sky over Battleship Row.

In one devastating split second, more than a thousand of *Arizona*'s men have been killed. The shock wave of the explosion crosses the harbor, a blast of such power that it sweeps men off the decks of the *Vestal, Nevada,* and *West Virginia.*

Rear Admiral Isaac Kidd and Captain Franklin Van Valkenburg, on *Arizona*'s bridge to direct defense, are instantly killed. As the smoke clears a bit, there is not one sign of life on her shattered, charred, and burning decks.

About this time, Admiral Kimmel, already ruined and facing further disgrace, reaches his head-quarters. He is far too late to do anything but hear and watch the disaster unfold, and only hope that the casualties won't be too high. The defensive battle is up to the men on the guns, and he can do nothing personally to aid them. Beyond that, he can only search for the enemy if he has any aircraft still undamaged.

Bombs keep on falling. *Maryland* is hit by two, and U.S.S. *Tennessee,* moored inboard of the now-sunken *West Virginia,* staggers as three crash into her decks.

Across the channel from Battleship Row, at the naval station's dock, the *Helena* is fighting to stay afloat. *Oglala,* alongside her, is sinking but not from a direct hit. The impact of the torpedo that struck *Helena* has opened *Oglala's* ancient seams, and now she is like a sieve.

Around on the other side of Ford Island, the bulky old target ship *Utah,* struck on the first wave of torpedo bombers, is listing heavily, and water laps along her port side, almost at her main deck. *Raleigh,* astern of her, also has a port list, and water has penetrated her boiler rooms.

On devastated *Arizona* there are now some signs of life. Men, some burned critically, most dazed and in shock, begin to crawl out of twisted hatches and from smashed gun turrets. There are not many

of them, but a few make it aboard the wreckage of
the *Vestal,* still laced to the destroyed battleship.

The *Vestal*'s skipper, Commander Cassin Young,
blown into the fiery water, swims back to his ship
and clambers aboard. He's determined to save her,
if possible. He orders the lines to the *Arizona* to be
chopped. He hails a passing Navy tug and prepares
to have the *Vestal* towed to an anchorage on the
other side of the harbor.

Another ship is under way, guns fully manned, leaving behind the flames and smoke of Pearl Harbor. She is U.S.S. *Helm,* the only vessel on the move when the first bomb fell. Now she is standing out to sea at twenty-seven knots, ready to take on anything that might come over the horizon.

It is 8:17 A.M. as she clears the harbor entrance. Immediately *Helm* spots one of the midget submarines, about a thousand yards away. The nose of the little craft seems to be up on a coral bank near the entrance buoys. The destroyer's guns open up but the midget slides off the coral reef unharmed. It submerges as *Helm* radios: "Small Jap submarine trying to penetrate harbor."

While the *Helm* is engaging the midget U-boat, the B-17's from California, the flight destined for the Philippines, are attempting to land at any field that looks halfway clear. As early as 8:00 A.M. they began their approaches to Oahu.

They've been up almost fourteen hours, and all are running low on gas, having flown to their extreme range. In fact, Lieutenant Barthlemes, skipper of one of the four-engined bombers, had thoughts of ditching his aircraft because of fuel shortage. Then he saw a group of planes out there with him. An escort, no doubt, he thought. Yet, on closer look, the "escort" had red "meatballs" painted on its fuselages.

Major Truman Landon had seen nine planes earlier. He discovered they were enemy when one fired a machine-gun burst at his B-17. Now, at 8:20, he is landing at Hickam with three Japanese fighters on his tail. One B-17 lands with its after section burning. Several others pick small airfields that do not seem to be under attack.

Pilots off the American carrier *Enterprise* are not quite so fortunate. She had launched eighteen aircraft at 6:15 A.M. while the big flat-top was about two hundred miles away from Oahu, returning from her delivery trip to Wake Island. The planes were to scout ahead of *Enterprise* and then land at Ford Island.

None of the pilots were aware of the attack until about 8:00 A.M., when they were converging on Oahu. Five have been shot down, either by Japanese aircraft or antiaircraft fire from the ground. Three pilots have been killed. The other planes crash-land or make it into Ford or Ewa, dodging fire from the U.S. Navy.

Even civilian planes become entangled with the Japanese. Three small aircraft manage to come face-to-face with one or another enemy groups, and two of them are fired on.

Lieutenant Commander Fuchida's mission is now nearing an end, but a second wave of Japanese planes, 170 of them under Lieutenant Commander Shigekazu Shimazaki, are boring toward Kahuku Point. They will come in to blast at whatever ships are still floating, and will hammer away again at Ford Island and Hickam Field.

At about 8:25, after a final hit on *California,* Fuchida's group begins to head north, but the commander himself decides to stay around and take photographs of the damage, then watch Shimazaki's planes make their attack. There is still no air opposition from the Americans that he can see, and he climbs to 15,000 feet.

While the main action for the last few minutes has been around Pearl Harbor and Hickam, dive-bombers have hit Kaneohe again, and Zeros have struck at Ewa, at Bellows Field, and even at little Haleiwa Field, scarcely noticeable from the air, after two B-17's have made emergency landings there.

Then, a little past 8:30 A.M., the enemy seems to vanish from the skies over Oahu, leaving behind the coils of black smoke and flames arising from its naval base and airfields.

He does not vanish from the waters, though. Coming in at this moment for a torpedo attack is a Japanese midget sub. She's moving up toward the west side of Ford Island. The sub is spotted first by the U.S.S. *Breese,* a destroyer-minelayer; then sighted by personnel aboard the U.S.S. *Curtiss* and U.S.S. *Medusa.*

Heading down the west channel is the destroyer U.S.S. *Monaghan,* and all three ships warn *Monaghan.* She's practically bow-on to the tiny undersea craft. The *Curtiss'* first shots thud into the conning tower, and the *Monaghan* opens up at pointblank range as the sub fires its two torpedoes.

One streaks by the *Curtiss,* and the other misses the *Monaghan,* both exploding on hitting the Ford Island shore. As the *Monaghan* tries to ram, her bow glances off the sub's conning tower. Slewing around, the midget bangs against *Monaghan*'s hull and rolls off in her wake as depth-charges, set for shallow explosion, ignite. They crush the little sub instantly.

Cheers ring out, as they had when the *Nevada* gunners got the torpedo plane. It is a small victory on this day of defeat, but a victory nonetheless.

The *Monaghan* steams on out to sea.

So far, the midget subs have yet to score. But in one, at least, the men are still trying. Ensign Sakamaki and Petty Officer Inagaki, having finally gotten under way after their compass troubles, and having survived one depth-charging already, are again moving toward the Pearl Harbor entrance, determined to destroy a ship.

THE SECOND WAVE

13

It is only a short period, the lull between attacks—perhaps ten minutes at most when the skies are clear of enemy aircraft—and somehow Pearl Harbor begins to recover. There are signs of it everywhere. Men wait by their guns now for the enemy to return. They know he will.

The *Nevada* is trying to get under way; preparations are being made to move the sinking *Oglala* from the *Helena*'s side. The *Vestal* is nearing a safer anchorage at Aiea. There is still chaos, still havoc; men are still being pulled from the burning, debris-littered waters; but a change of mood is in the air. It is now an angry *fight back!*

Over in the Navy Yard, Captain Charles Cooke of U.S.S. *Pennsylvania,* which is under repair and sitting in the drydock, orders the dock gates to be opened partially. Behind him, perched on chocks, are the destroyers *Cassin* and *Downes.* If the drydock is suddenly ruptured, his big *Pennsylvania* will crush the small destroyers in the flood of harbor waters. Meanwhile they sit ready, guns manned.

Most amazing of all is U.S.S. *Nevada*. Torpedoed and bombed in the first wave, she's almost ready to sail. At sea, at least, she can maneuver instead of being a sitting duck on Battleship Row.

Perhaps most amazed are *Nevada*'s own men. They'd always been told it took at least two hours to get up enough steam to power her engine turbines. Now, in just forty-five minutes, that steam is up. In the past she had always needed four tugs to help her sail or dock. Now she is getting under way without any assistance.

What's more, neither her captain nor her executive officer, the number two in command, is aboard. The daring decision to run from Battleship Row has been made by a reserve officer, Lieutenant Commander Francis Thomas. Normally he is *Nevada*'s damage-control officer, in charge of directing emergency repairs.

On the bridge with Thomas will be a cool, steady veteran of ship handling, Chief Quartermaster Robert Sedberry. But Sedberry has never faced a task like this, threading the behemoth downstream under almost certain enemy attack.

Nevada is cast off, partially hidden by the coiling black smoke over Battleship Row. She moves slowly and steadily past the twisted *Arizona* at about 8:40 A.M. Again, there are cheers from other ships, and from the oil-stained, half-naked survivors standing along the shore of Ford Island. The Stars and Stripes flutters from her stern. Guns aboard her point skyward. *Nevada* is suddenly a symbol of defiance.

Such a symbol is desperately needed. A moment later, the enemy roars in again. There are fifty-four high-level Kate bombers, eighty Val dive-bombers, and thirty-six Zero fighters in this second wave led by Commander Shimazaki.

The high-level Kates have the first mission, going in to drop bombs on the *Tennessee* and *West Virginia*. Six planes are in the first attack run, and then a group of nine planes start their runs across the Navy Yard toward Battleship Row. A third group of nine planes begins to concentrate on the big drydock holding *Pennsylvania,* with the destroyers *Cassin* and *Downes* locked in behind her.

Guns boom out from every sector of Pearl Harbor, from the destroyer nests in the far reaches to the Navy Yard drydocks. The sky is peppered with black bursts of shell fire.

Fuchida's planes had run into very little ack-ack. It's a different story now. Gun barrels become so hot that paint peels off them. The defense is a furious one. In the heat of it, some shells land in Hono-

lulu, causing civilian casualties and minor damage.

On the cruiser *New Orleans,* which has been undergoing minor overhaul at the naval station berths facing Southeast Loch, electric power from shore has been disrupted and ammunition has to be passed hand to hand instead of on mechanical lifts. Then a legend is born: Chaplain Howell Forgy, unable to participate in the fighting because he is a minister, stands on the deck to encourage the ammunition passers. Slapping their sweaty backs, he shouts, "Praise the Lord, and pass the ammunition!" Later it is revealed that these words—popularized in a hit war song—are not exactly what he said, but they are a true indication of the spirit that was there.

The enemy aircraft sight *Nevada,* now clearing Battleship Row, and swarm over to her. *Nevada*'s guns send up a barrage of steel, and she's almost hidden from both air and shore view by the smoke from her barrels.

A bomb hits her, then another. Flames and flying metal cover her superstructure. A third bomb slams into her on the starboard side. She shudders but keeps moving. An estimated thirty bombers are now concentrating on *Nevada.* Near-misses send spouts of water into the air around her as Sedberry weaves her past a dredge pipeline that extends halfway into the channel.

The Japanese pilots see a chance to sink her in the channel, perhaps blocking the harbor for months to come. On shore, senior officers watching her escape through binoculars anticipate this strategy.

Flags break out from the 14th Naval District signal tower: *Keep clear of the channel!*

If Thomas and Sedberry can't use the channel, their gallant voyage is over; the *Nevada* can't go to sea.

At about 9:00 A.M. Thomas orders all engines stopped, and Sedberry swings her bow toward Hospital Point, nosing into the mud. The anchor is dropped, and *Nevada*'s short run to open ocean is ended. Taking water, her bridge and superstructure afire, *Nevada*'s guns are still firing as a final bomb explodes near her bow.

Shimazaki's aircraft now turn to targets that have been ignored during *Nevada*'s sprint. Bombs begin to fall on the *Pennsylvania, Downes,* and *Cassin* in the drydock, which is almost flooded when the *Pennsy* takes her first hit shortly after nine. While she is the target, the destroyers take most of the near-misses. In a moment both are burning stem to stern. *Pennsylvania* shakes again after a direct hit.

At 9:12 the destroyer *Shaw,* in the floating drydock nearby, is hit and blazes up. The seaplane tender *Curtiss,* anchored off Pearl City, is next to be plastered; then the cruiser *Honolulu,* at Southeast Loch.

The *Shaw*'s fire has reached her forward magazines, and at 9:30 the whole blackened sky over the Navy Yard turns red as the destroyer explodes. Over the mushroom of the fireball are red and white streaks as shells fly up and explode. One crosses the channel to fall on Ford Island.

At 9:37 a massive explosion on the *Cassin* shatters her hull, and she rolls over on the already stricken *Downes.* It is the final big explosion of the morning.

While the ships have again been the principal targets for Lieutenant Commander Shimazaki's crack pilots, Japanese aircraft have also been putting in appearances over Hickam, Ford Island, and Wheeler. The Zero fighter cover has strafed Hickam and Kaneohe as well.

But this time there is some opposition in the air. What it lacks in size it makes up in courage. When group leader Lieutenant Sakamaki's planes swept through Kolekole Pass to strafe Wheeler Field, U.S. Army Air Corps Lieutenants George Welch and Kenneth Taylor had piled into a car for a dash to Haleiwa Field, a small auxiliary strip on the northwest coast. Their P-40 fighter aircraft were parked there. They had called ahead to have crewmen ram in belts of ammunition for their machine guns. The aircraft were already gassed up.

Welch and Taylor took off at about eight thirty hunting for the enemy, and flew to Barber's Point. By that time Fuchida's planes were finishing up attacks over Pearl and Hickam, and heading north again.

So Welch and Taylor flew back to Wheeler for more ammunition, and were off the ground at about 9:00 A.M., airborne at almost the same time nine Japanese strafers came to pay a final visit to the field.

Within a minute they had downed two enemy planes. Heading for Ewa, where dive-bombers were

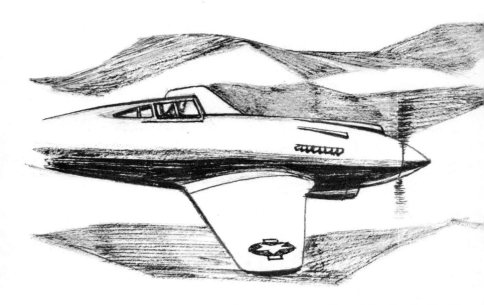

operating, they got four more. After Taylor's P-40 was hit with machine-gun fire, forcing him to earth, Welch managed to shoot down another Val.

Although there were earlier attempts to scramble fighters from Wheeler, and later attempts, during Shimazaki's second wave, to send them up from Bellows, only Taylor and Welch are credited with air kills this Sunday.

At about 9:45 A.M. Fuchida watches as the last of Shimazaki's planes disappear toward the north. With the gas load in his Kate, he can stay around a bit longer to make final observations for reporting to Vice-Admiral Nagumo.

Fuchida is confident that most of the heavy ships in Pearl Harbor have been sunk, or severely damaged. He knows that practically all the aircraft on Oahu have been destroyed. Yet there are targets still untouched. Although he does not know his own losses, he feels that they are not great. (Actually, he has lost three Zero fighters, a dive-bomber, and five torpedo planes. Shimazaki's losses, due to increased antiaircraft fire and the P-40 action of Welch and Taylor, have been larger: six fighters and fourteen dive-bombers.)

The Japanese carriers have now moved to within 190 miles of Pearl Harbor to recover their aircraft, and at about 10:00 A.M. the first of Fuchida's early attack groups begin arriving, many of the fighters low on gas. As soon as they land, those not severely damaged are refueled and rearmed for the possibility of a third strike.

Three hundred and twenty-four planes return from both waves. Twenty-nine have been lost, with a loss of fifty-five personnel.

Fuchida stays on above Oahu until shortly after 10:00 A.M. and then sets course back for the carriers, landing after 11:00 A.M. He reports immediately to Vice-Admiral Nagumo, listing the damage that he believes has been inflicted on the American fleet. Then he urges another attack.

Commander Genda is opposed. He does not believe it is worth the risk. Antiaircraft opposition will be even greater next time, and the absence of the American carriers is on his mind. They are somewhere at sea, and Genda has no desire to engage them in battle. Hitting them in the confines of Pearl Harbor would be one thing, a duel with them on the high seas is another. Why risk it? Then too, radio interceptions indicate there are still American bombers on Oahu that can be launched.

Nagumo listens to the reports of the other flight commanders, and when Rear Admiral Ryunosuke Kusaka, his chief of staff, sides with Genda in opposing a third wave, Nagumo makes his decision.

It is 1:30 P.M. when the admiral signals to the task force to retire at top speed to the north.

This decision does not surprise Admiral Yamamoto, on board the *Nagato* in the Inland Sea. In fact, only moments before, he had predicted it. Both Nagumo and Kusaka had originally opposed the raid because of its risks, and now, after apparent success, their natural reaction is to retire, not stage another raid.

When Fuchida departed from the skies over Oahu, the only enemy still left to operate was beneath the sea. Some of the Japanese submarines were still in the vicinity, having seen no action, but due for an interesting day. United States destroyers *Dale, Blue, Aylwin, Henley,* and *Phelp* were now at sea and hunting for signs of the raiders.

The cruisers *St. Louis, Detroit,* and *Phoenix* were also under way, ready to engage if any Japanese ships could be sighted.

Ensign Sakamaki and Petty Officer Inagaki, in their midget craft, continue a day of floundering, are rendered unconscious by fumes in the drifting U-boat, and are finally grounded during the night, far away from Pearl Harbor. At dawn the next day, they abandon the little craft. Inagaki drowns, but Sakamaki makes it to the beach near Bellows Field to become the first Japanese prisoner of war taken by the United States.

A DATE THAT WILL LIVE
IN INFAMY

14

At 10:00 A.M. no one in Pearl Harbor, or anywhere on Oahu, knows that the enemy is retreating. In fact, they await another attack on the ships and airfields. Rumors spread that the Japanese have troop transports off Barber's Point; one radio broadcast says Japanese troops have already landed. Other word spreads that paratroopers are dropping, enemy battleships have been sighted, Japanese saboteurs are at work. False reports come in all day.

While this is going on, men are still being picked out of the oily harbor waters. Ambulances are rushing to hospitals with the wounded; boats are going alongside the mercy ship *Solace* with burned and wounded. Officers and men caught on shore when the attack started are rushing back to their ships by any means of transportation. Some have no ships to go to, and join in with rescue or salvage work.

The *Nevada* is pulled off the mud at Hospital

Point about ten o'clock and beached on Waipio Point, across the channel. With her nose on the beach, the Japanese cannot possibly sink her to block the harbor entrance.

At about the same time, the old *Oglala* gives up and rolls on its side. "Abandon ship" is called out on the *West Virginia*. There is nothing more her men can do. The *California* is also abandoned at 10:02, but less than fifteen minutes later Captain Bunkley recalls the crew to fight fires and save the ship.

Over on *Utah,* lying on its side, there are tappings from the hull. They can mean only one thing —men are still trapped inside her. Even as the second wave of Japanese planes gains altitude to the north, *Utah* survivors clamber back on the slippery steel. Then sailors from *Raleigh* and *Tangier* arrive with cutting equipment.

It is the same on *Oklahoma,* her bottom to the sky. Navy Yard workmen join with sailors to open holes. They listen to the tapping, locate its source, and then tap back. Blue arcs of acetylene torches slice at the hull, but the men soon find that the gas torches eat up oxygen inside the ship. They switch to pneumatic equipment, driven by compressed air. Thirty-six hours later, when no more taps can be heard, thirty-two of *Oklahoma's* men have been saved from certain death.

There are three men deep inside *West Virginia.* Long after the fires are put out on her decks and in her compartments, they are known to be alive, yet no one can reach them. Not until Christmas Eve, though, are all hopes of saving them abandoned.

Two men trapped in the *California* have better luck. They are brought out at 3:00 P.M.

Throughout the island—at Wheeler, Ewa Hickam, Kaneohe, Bellows, and at Schofield Barracks, the immediate task is to get medical aid for the wounded and injured, put out the fires, clear away debris, and get ready to fight again. Troops are being moved to bolster defenses; ammunition is being resupplied to guns. The *Pennsylvania* points her heavy batteries toward the harbor entrance in case the Japanese return by sea.

If Premier Tojo had expected the Americans to give up—their will to fight broken by the surprise raids—he might have been disheartened to see what was occurring on Oahu after 10:00 A.M.

Through the movement of troops, past roadblocks, and through the general confusion, a young Japanese named Tadeo Fuchikama is riding an Indian motorcycle on his rounds, delivering RCA cables. He has a number to deliver, and although he knows the Japanese have attacked, the cables must be distributed as on any other day. He has been on his route since shortly after 8:00 A.M.

One cable is addressed to the Commanding General at headquarters, Fort Shafter. Fuchikama, noting that it has not been marked urgent or given any other priority, has placed it in his pouch for routine handling. The cable arrived in Honolulu at 7:33 A.M., more than twenty minutes before the first bomb fell.

Yet it is well after eleven o'clock, when Fuchikama has delivered practically all the other cables, that he arrives at Fort Shafter. About three o'clock the cable reaches General Short. He reads it, and then, without comment, orders it relayed to Admiral Kimmel.

This message from General Marshall, the last-minute "war warning" to Hawaii, is late, tragically late.

Admiral Kimmel reads it and then tosses it into a wastebasket. General Marshall's mishandled warning isn't of the slightest interest any more.

At 11:27 four Army B-26 bombers are airborne to search for the enemy carriers. They go north, but not very far, and find no trace of the Japanese fleet. A few minutes after noon, nine of *Enterprise*'s undamaged aircraft are launched to search the north. They fly out about 200 miles, but Nagumo has already vanished into the gray mists.

As the *Enterprise* aircraft lift off from Ford Island, the pilots can see the devastation. Smoke is still rising from all the battered airfields, but the fires on the runways, in the hangars and barracks, have been extinguished. Battleship Row is blanketed in thick smoke, and the oil-fed flames on *Arizona* will continue to burn for several days.

Lost are the battleships *Arizona* and *Oklahoma,* the target ship *Utah,* the destroyers *Cassin* and *Downes.* The *West Virginia* and *California* are sunk, and the *Nevada* beached to keep it from sinking.

The battleships *Tennessee, Maryland,* and *Pennsylvania* are damaged, as are the cruisers *Helena, Honolulu,* and *Raleigh,* the destroyer *Shaw,* the seaplane tender *Curtiss,* and the *Vestal.* But all except *Arizona, Oklahoma, Utah, Cassin,* and *Downes* will rejoin the fleet after urgent repair work. Three of the damaged battleships will put out to sea in less than two weeks.

Destroyed are 96 Army aircraft, and 92 Navy and Marine aircraft, with another 159 damaged.

Worst of all, the human cost! A total of 2,403 people have been killed, of which 68 are civilians. Another 1,178 sailors, soldiers, and civilians have been wounded or injured.

But Pearl Harbor is only a part of Japan's strategy to conquer Asia and turn the Pacific into a Nipponese stronghold. Radio reports of attack are coming in from Hong Kong, from Thailand, from the

Malay Peninsula. Japan has struck on a line that stretches from the Gulf of Siam to Hawaii. Manila is bombed! Soon Midway, Wake, and Guam islands will be under attack.

Japan has launched her war on a wide front, confident that she can achieve her aims in all of Asia as well as the Pacific now that the United States fleet in Hawaii has been disabled. There is great rejoicing in Tokyo as news of the Pearl Harbor destruction is announced.

The Japanese have not thought too much about America's industrial might or its abilities to come back from early defeat and wage war. In fact, in the hours following announcement of the attack, few Japanese seem to consider the possibility that the Pacific fleet might well be rebuilt, strengthened, and sail again.

About eighteen hours after the *Enterprise* planes take off in their futile attempt to find the enemy task force, President Roosevelt stands before a joint session of Congress to ask for formal declaration of war against the Japanese Empire.

He begins: "Yesterday, December 7, a date which will live in infamy, the United States of America was suddenly and deliberately attacked . . . ."

Congress responds to his request, and the United States enters World War II, as war is also declared on Germany and Italy, the Axis partners of Japan.

THE HEROES AND THE SCAPEGOATS

15

Not until after the battle is over, after the guns are stilled, are the stories of heroism made known. Even then, countless deeds of individual courage and self-sacrifice are never told. Surely there were heroic moments among those trapped below decks in *Arizona, Oklahoma,* and *Utah,* split-seconds of gallantry that will remain forever unknown.

But as the hours pass, as the combat-weary survivors exchange experiences and tell of what they have seen and heard, the stories ebb and flow. It has been this way since the beginning of mankind, after the conflict. This is how legends are born.

Pearl Harbor has its legendary figures, as had the Alamo with Davy Crockett and Jim Bowie. Pearl Harbor has some of the spirit of Captain Lawrence of U.S.S. *Chesapeake* in the War of 1812. Dying, he called out, "Don't give up the ship!"

Aviation Chief Ordnanceman John Finn was on

the ramps at Kaneohe Naval Air Station as the first wave of attackers roared in, wing guns peppering the parked aircraft. Picking up a loaded machine gun, Finn raced across the ramp to mount it on a stand.

Bullets laced the earth near him as he began to fire back. Alone, out on the exposed ramp, Finn had no protection from the strafing planes, yet his gun kept chattering even after he was wounded.

Finn's citation for the Medal of Honor, the nation's highest military award, tells the story:

> Although painfully wounded many times, he continued to man his gun and to return the enemy fire vigorously, and with telling effect throughout the enemy strafing and bombing attack, and with complete disregard to his own personal safety. It was only after specific orders that he was persuaded to leave his post to seek medical attention. Following first aid treatment, although obviously suffering much pain and moving with great difficulty, he returned to his squadron area and actively supervised the rearming of returning planes. His extraordinary heroism and conduct in this action are considered to be in accord with the highest traditions of the Naval Service.

Ensign Herbert Jones, assisting on an ammunition-passing detail for the topside guns, was mortally wounded when a Japanese bomb exploded deep in *California*'s hull. His wounded mates attempted to carry him out, but he ordered, "Leave me alone. I'm done for. Get out of here before the magazines go off."

Also on *California,* Machinist's Mate Robert R. Scott was manning the compressors that supplied the topside guns with blasts of cleaning air after each round was fired. When a torpedo ruptured the hull, spewing oil and water in, Scott shouted, "This is my station. I'll stay here and give them air as long as the guns are going."

The steel door was slammed to prevent water from flooding the entire ship. Scott kept the compressors going until they were underwater. He died beside them.

When the *Nevada* was ready to cast off her lines and dash out for the open sea, Chief Boatswain Edwin Hill climbed down to the quay and cut her loose. Then he dove into the water and swam to catch up with her. Thirty minutes later, after she grounded at Hospital Point, Hill was laboring to drop her anchor when the bomb exploded off her bow. He was blown overboard and killed instantly.

Another veteran chief petty officer, Peter Tomich, in the *Utah,* calmly went about his work in the engineering spaces as the ship capsized. First he made certain that all personnel in the boiler room had cleared out, and then he secured the boilers so they wouldn't explode, adding further damage to the ship. He gave his life.

In the same vessel Fireman 2nd Class John Vaessen remained at his post, keeping the lights going until the last second, so that men below decks might find their way out. After the ship rolled over, Vaessen took a flashlight and a wrench and found his way to the dynamo room. He knew the general location of a manhole that would lead to the ship's double bottom. Soon Vaessen was tapping on the steel with his wrench. Sailors cut a hole from the outside, and he crawled to safety.

Negro Doris Miller, huge and powerful mess steward in the *West Virginia,* helped carry his mortally wounded commanding officer, Captain Mervyn Bennion, to a place that was sheltered and then manned a machine gun. Trained for kitchen work and serving, as were most nonwhite personnel in the Navy at that time, Miller had no experience in gunnery, but he found the trigger and blazed away, laying down a harassing fire.

His action proved, once again, that heroism is a matter of individual courage and has nothing to do with race or color. He later gave his life in a carrier battle. Before the war was over, the Navy began to change its policy of automatically designating Negroes as mess stewards. Miller's heroism helped.

Miller was awarded the Navy Cross for his performance at Pearl Harbor, and Captain Bennion, requesting reports on the action until his last breath, concerned only for his ship, received the Medal of Honor, posthumously.

Catholic Chaplain Aloysius Schmitt helped four men escape through a porthole of the *Oklahoma* as she capsized, but there wasn't enough time to save his own life. Chief Watertender Francis Day assisted fifteen men to safety through a submerged porthole, sacrificing himself. Ensign Francis Flaherty and Seaman James Ward helped others escape from one of *Oklahoma*'s big gun turrets, resting on Pearl's murky bottom, but did not have the same luck.

Perhaps the story of Marine Sergeant Tom Hailey, among the survivors, best demonstrates the determination of the men of Pearl Harbor. Captain of *Oklahoma*'s No. 10 broadside 5-inch gun, Hailey was in his bunk when the first torpedo struck. Before he could reach his gun the ship capsized, and Hailey dove into the water, swimming to the *Maryland*.

He climbed aboard *Maryland*, saw an antiaircraft gun not completely manned, rounded up a crew, and began firing. A bomb hit scattered Hailey's crew; then smoke and fire made it impossible to operate the gun. So the sergeant dove into the harbor again.

Reporting to the air station, he volunteered his services for whatever tasks were needed. Within a few minutes Hailey was seated in an amphibian aircraft, an old Springfield rifle in his hands. For the next five hours he flew as a lookout while the pilot searched for the Japanese fleet.

A total of fourteen officers and enlisted men received the Medal of Honor; fifty-two were awarded the Navy Cross; four received Silver Stars, and four the Navy and Marine Corps Medal.

Not all the heroes of Pearl Harbor were military personnel. Crane operator George Walters, perched high in his cab above the drydock where *Pennsylvania* sat, became so enraged at the attack that he attempted to fight the enemy aircraft with his crane, swinging the big hook back and forth to spoil the runs of the dive-bombers and fighters.

Civilian machinist Henry Danner became an ammunition passer on the *Pennsylvania.* Other civilians helped fill ammunition belts, fight fires, clear up bomb damage, and assist in harbor rescues.

Undoubtedly, many acts of gallantry, both military and civilian, went unrecognized.

There were those in Washington and in Hawaii, at the highest levels of government and in the highest ranks of the military, who had made tragic, costly, almost unbelievable mistakes. There were also those

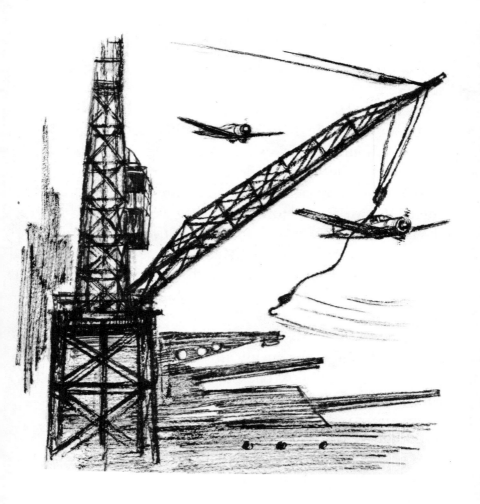

in lesser positions and of lesser ranks who contributed to the disaster and defeat at Pearl Harbor.

While Admiral Kimmel and General Short were relieved of their duties in Hawaii, and Admiral Stark sent on to other duties, as were several other high-ranking officers in Washington, the blame for

Pearl Harbor cannot fall solely on Kimmel and Short. Too many, from President Roosevelt on down, were deeply involved in bad judgment and gross negligence.

Lengthy hearings by several Congressional committees went far beyond Kimmel and Short in establishing negligence, but a number of questions concerning Pearl Harbor, and particularly White House involvements, have not been answered to this day, and may never be answered. Certain documents simply "disappeared." For example, the crucial "Execute the Winds" message vanished from the files.

At the time of the hearings, and later, there was some opinion, voiced by members of Congress, military writers, and columnists, that Kimmel and Short were the "scapegoats" of Pearl Harbor, the men who were forced to take more than their share of the blame for the disaster. Kimmel, bitter to the day of his death, in turn placed a major share of the blame on Admiral Stark.

President Roosevelt's personal involvement has long been a matter of sharp and divided opinion. There were, and are, those who feel he might have prevented the surprise element of the attack by making certain his military commanders in the field knew of the events being revealed by Magic. Harsher judgment says he welcomed the attack because it permitted entry into World War II, a step that even his most ardent critics acknowledge as inevitable.

His defenders, in the political majority, claim that he had no more idea that the Japanese would strike Pearl Harbor than did Kimmel or Short. If anything, they maintain, he was a victim of lack of information and good judgment from his subordinates.

In testimony before the Joint Congressional Committee in January 1946, Admiral Kimmel said:

> Assuming that for the first time on December 5 I had all the important information then available in the Navy Department, it is my conviction that I would have gone to sea with the fleet, including the carrier *Lexington,* and arranged a rendezvous at sea with Halsey's carrier force, and been in good position to intercept the Japanese attack.
>
> . . . Even on the morning of December 7, four or five hours before the attack, had the Navy Department for the first time seen fit to send me all this significant information, and the additional fact that 1 P.M., Washington time, had been fixed for the delivery of the Japanese ultimatum to the United States, my light forces could have moved out of Pearl Harbor, all ships in the harbor would have been at general quarters, and all resources of the fleet in instant readiness to repel an attack . . . .

Answering the same committee, General Short said:

I do not feel that I have been fairly treated, or with justice, by the War Department. I was singled out as an example, as the scapegoat, for the disaster. My relatively small part in the transaction was not explained to the American people until this joint congressional committee forced the revelation of the facts. I fully appreciate the desire of the War Department to preserve the secrecy of the source of the so-called "Magic," but I am sure that could have been done without any attempt to deceive the public by a false pretense that my judgment had been the sole factor causing the failure of the Army to fulfill its mission of defending the Navy at Pearl Harbor. I am sure that an honest confession by the War Department General Staff of their failure to anticipate the surprise raid would have been understood by the public, in the long run, and even at the time. Instead, they "passed the buck" to me, and I have kept my silence until the opportunity of this public forum was presented to me. . . .

It was a rather pathetic summary—words for history—but also words for thought for those who would administer the nation's defenses in the future. By the time of the hearings, 1946, the war with Japan had been won. She had surrendered after atom-bomb attacks on two of her islands.

Actually, Japan had fought a losing battle for a long time before the nuclear blasts at Nagasaki and Hiroshima. The tide of battle had turned at Midway

Island in June 1942, when Vice-Admiral Nagumo's carrier forces were routed. *Soryu, Akagi, Kaga,* and *Hiryu,* ships that had raided Pearl Harbor, were destroyed. Yamamoto's once-proud force never recovered.

Pearl Harbor obviously did not achieve for Japan what she had hoped. History has assessed it as a classic military blunder. Even tactically it proved to be a blunder because the Japanese did not destroy the ship-repair facilities at the naval base, the huge oil-storage tanks, the ammunition magazines, or the submarine base. The submarines went out to sink enemy ships by the dozens. The carriers, at sea, were untouched.

Within six months, the Pacific Fleet was stronger and larger than it had been when Commander Fuchida victoriously signaled, "Tora! Tora! Tora!" It grew to gigantic proportions and eventually sank almost every fighting ship in the Imperial Fleet.

As the events at Fortress Alamo in 1836 and the sinking of the U.S.S. *Maine* in Havana in 1898 had rallied the American people with cries of "Remember the Alamo," and "Remember the *Maine,*" the slogan "Remember Pearl Harbor" was to serve the American nation as a call to arms, and finally, victory.

KEY FIGURES IN THE STORY OF PEARL HARBOR

Generalissimo Chiang Kai-shek: leader of the Chinese military forces in the war with Japan at the time of the attack on Pearl Harbor and later President of the national government of China.

Commander Minoru Genda: the man primarily responsible for formulating and executing the detailed plans for the Japanese air strike on Pearl Harbor.

Joseph C. Grew: United States ambassador to Japan.

Hirohito: Emperor of Japan.

Cordell Hull: United States secretary of state.

Admiral Husband Kimmel: Commander-in-chief of the United States Navy's Pacific Fleet and the highest-ranking naval officer in Hawaii at the time of the attack.

Nagao Kita: Japanese consul general in Honolulu.

Frank Knox: United States secretary of the navy.

Saburo Kurusu: Japanese ambassador to Washington.

General George C. Marshall: chief of staff of the United States Army during World War II, the highest-ranking Army officer.

Admiral Osami Nagano: chief of staff of the Imperial Japanese Navy, the highest-ranking naval officer.

Vice-Admiral Chuichi Nagumo: commander of the Japanese task force that attacked Pearl Harbor.

Admiral Kichisaburo Nomura: Japanese ambassador to Washington.

Franklin D. Roosevelt: President of the United States.

Lieutenant General Walter Short: chief United States Army commander in Hawaii at the time of the attack.

Admiral Harold Stark: chief of naval operations, the highest position in the United States Navy.

Henry Stimson: United States secretary of war.

General Hideki Tojo: Japan's minister of war, who in 1941 became prime minister.

Admiral Isoroku Yamamoto: commander-in-chief of the Combined Fleet of the Imperial Japanese Navy and the man who conceived and directed the surprise attack on Pearl Harbor.

Takeo Yoshikawa: ensign in the Imperial Japanese Navy and an important spy, responsible for providing Tokyo with information about American military installations in Hawaii.

BIBLIOGRAPHY

ALLEN, GWENFREAD. *Hawaii's War Years, 1941–1945*. Honolulu: University of Hawaii Press, 1945.

BATESON, CHARLES. *War with Japan: A Concise History*. East Lansing: Michigan State University Press, 1968.

BEASLEY, W. G. *The Modern History of Japan*. New York: Frederick A. Praeger, 1963.

BROWNE, COURTNEY. *Tojo, the Last Banzai*. New York: Holt, Rinehart, and Winston, 1967.

DAVIS, BURKE. *Get Yamamoto*. New York: Random House, 1969.

DAVIS, FOREST. *How War Came*. New York: Simon & Schuster, 1942.

FARAGO, LADISLAS. *The Broken Seal*. New York: Random House, 1967.

FEIS, HERBERT. *The Road to Pearl Harbor*. Princeton, N. J.: Princeton University Press, 1950.

FLOWER, DESMOND, and REEVES, JAMES, Editors. *The Taste of Courage: The War, 1939–1945*. New York: Harper & Brothers, 1960.

HASHIMOTO, MOCHITSURA. *Sunk*. New York: Henry Holt & Co., 1954.

HOEHLING, A. A. *The Week Before Pearl Harbor*. New York: W. W. Norton & Co., 1963.

KARIG, COMMANDER WALTER, USNR, and KELLY, LIEUTENANT WELBOURN, USNR. *Battle Report, Pearl Harbor to Coral Sea*. New York: Farrar & Rinehart, Inc., 1944.

KIMMEL, ADMIRAL HUSBAND E. *Admiral Kimmel's Story*. Chicago: Henry Regnery Co., 1955.

LORD, WALTER. *Day of Infamy*. New York: Henry Holt & Co., 1957.

MILLIS, WALTER. *This Is Pearl*. New York: William Morrow & Co., 1947.

MORGENSTERN, GEORGE. *Pearl Harbor, the Story of the Secret War*. New York: The Devin-Adair Co., 1947.

MORISON, REAR ADMIRAL SAMUEL ELIOT. *History of United States Naval Operations in World War II.* Vol. III, *The Rising Sun in the Pacific.* Boston: Little, Brown & Co., 1961.

Pearl Harbor Attack. Hearings before the Joint Committee on the Investigation of the Pearl Harbor Attack, Congress of the United States, 79th Congress. Vols. 1-11. Washington, D. C.: Government Printing Office, 1946.

POTTER, JOHN DEANE. *Yamamoto.* New York: Paperback Library, 1967.

SMITH, S. E. *The United States Navy in World War II.* New York: William Morrow & Co., 1966.

THEOBALD, REAR ADMIRAL ROBERT A. *The Final Secret of Pearl.* New York: The Devin-Adair Co., 1954.

TOLAND, JOHN. *But Not in Shame.* New York: Random House, 1961.

TREFOUSSE, HANS LOUIS, Editor. *What Happened at Pearl Harbor: Documents Pertaining to the Japanese Attack of December 7, 1941, and its Background.* New York: Twayne Publishers, 1958.

Author's Note

Much additional data was obtained from magazines and news clippings as the result of research during a year's association with the filming of *Tora! Tora! Tora!,* the Japanese-American production about the raid on Pearl Harbor. Talks with Minoru Genda and Mitsuo Fuchida added perspective. Time spent at Battleship Row, Ford Island, Wheeler Field, and other installations, as well as flights over several of the attack routes, provided a fresh insight into the events. Time spent in Japan during the filming of Japanese sequences in Tokyo, Kyoto, and Kyushu also provided valuable insight as the re-created characters of Yamamoto, Genda, Fuchida, and Prince Konoye came alive. Walking the decks of the reconstructed *Nagato* and *Akagi* on Kyushu, and watching rebuilt Zeros, Kates, and Vals attack Battleship Row helped me reenter history as it happened.

INDEX

ABOUT THE AUTHOR

Theodore Taylor is especially well qualified to write this book, since as assistant to the producer of a film about Pearl Harbor, *Tora! Tora! Tora!,* made by companies in Japan and the United States, he spent more than a year doing extensive research on the story of December 7, 1941. Interviews with some of the men who participated in the event, including former Commander Minoru Genda, and trips to Japan and Pearl Harbor gave him valuable and fresh insights into the "day of infamy" and helped him to recreate the events leading up to it.

Mr. Taylor is the author of two previously published books for young people, *People Who Make Movies* and *The Cay,* which was selected by the American Library Association as a Notable Children's Book of 1969 and also won eight other awards. He lives in California with his wife and three children.

ABOUT THE ILLUSTRATOR

Witold T. Mars was born in Poland and was graduated from the Academy of Fine Arts in Warsaw. He went for further study to France and Italy and eventually decided to settle in the United States. Mr. Mars's "deep interest in the history of art and in the culture of the Western world," together with his travels to the European countries of artistic relevance, have enabled him to produce a fine variety of award-winning illustrated books. He has exhibited his paintings in Poland, Sweden, and Great Britain, and many of his works are in several state and private collections.

W. T. Mars now lives in Forest Hills, New York, with his wife.